Raw EMOTIONS

My Dear Nelson,
There no words to describe
my ♥ for you - thank you for
always being in my corner
and I hope this book inspires
you to shoot for the stars.

Love Always,
Betty

P.S.
I hope titi
is proud ♥

BEATRIZ APONTE

outskirts
press

Special Thanks

To: God all mighty, for having mercy on my soul and blessing me with this opportunity to achieve this still so surreal goal; for allowing me to bring to life this childhood dream.

To: My daughters (granddaughters), my drive and reasons for standing so strong; this book is proof there's no perfect way or expiration date on chasing your dreams. Living proof of when life knocks you down, you must instantly get back up and fight even harder; a reminder that anything is possible with hard work and determination. I love you girls with every beat of my heart, with every breath I take (don't ever forget it).

To: The Rooms (you know who you are), for helping me take full inventory of self and giving me hope through true acceptance and understanding of being a working progress; for encouraging me and giving me the enthusiasm to start and finish this project. For teaching me it's okay to put myself first, while exercising such feeling with faith that the rest would fall into place. (I love you peter more than words could say) thank you for not giving up on your sister and leading by example.

To: Maria Ester Flores (my titi) may she rest in peace, for loving me the way you did, for reminding me always how beautiful I am inside and out; for listening to me for hours genuinely interested in my writing, thoughts and ideas; for knowing my worth when I didn't; for keeping all my secrets; for always defending, watching over and feeding me; for being proud of me regardless of my hustle. In memory of all your love stories and advice, I love you.

To: Roberto Carlos Acevedo (my tito) may he rest in peace, for helping cope with my aunt's death; for showing me with actions that romance does exist; for reading and listening to everything I ever wrote; for telling me "Betty you got this". I loved you then, I love you now and I will always love you (A Forever Promise).

To: Joseph Monaco SNR (the best boss ever) may he rest in peace, for believing in me and challenging me to "dream big"; for telling me I can accomplish anything I work hard for. I miss you dearly and will never, ever forget all of our wonderful and meaningful conversations.

To: Aracelis Gonzalez (speedy), for telling me for years to believe in my skills as a writer and publish my poetry; for always listening and reading my deepest feelings and thoughts, but more important for respecting them even when you disagreed; for allowing me to be your sister too. I have always admired your strength and determination, I love you.

To: Angelica Nazario (angie), for being part of my original audience, for always listening to me without judgments; for having faith in me even on my worst day; for every single time you had my back while I was out there making ends meet; for allowing me to be your sister too. I have always admired your hustle and your very beautiful heart, I love you.

To: Jesenia Martinez (Jessie), for keeping my poetry safe while I went through my trials and tribulations (if you wouldn't have saved everything, this wouldn't be possible), for reminding me that my writing is not a curse full of pain, but has always been my passion. I will forever be grateful. Thank you for giving me your time and space in your home. I love you and always miss you.

To: Joannie Rodriguez Baez (my rock), for being real and wholeheartedly opening your doors for me whenever I needed to get away; for giving me space to meditate and write for days in my favorite "marquesina" inspired by the coquis in my beautiful island; for being my rock when I traveled to bury my tito. I will forever be indebted to you (mi Hermana, mi panuelo de lagrimas). I love you so much and will always be here for you.

To: Anderline Bredy (amber), for always positively lifting my spirit; for introducing me to Maya Angelou (the best birthday gift ever) was when I realized there's an audience for my pain, and through my writing I might be able to help someone like me; for taking the time to type one of my poems for the very first time, I will never forget finding it on my desk amazed thinking "wow", "I wrote this". Thank you for planting the seed to this vision many years ago. Thank you for believing in me. Thank you for never changing, I love you.

To: Xavier Omar Rios (X), for babysitting so I could go back to school; for listening and believing in my writing and ideas; for drying my tears when no one else would; for never saying no to me. I love you like a brother (we are more than family).

To: Nelson Gonzalez (nelsito), you have always listened and supported me even through mail; thank you for always pointing out my good qualities when I'm down and out. You are an amazing soul just like your mother. I love you, miss you and can't wait to spend some quality time with you (dinner and a movie).

To: Ramsey J'oel Martinez (my ecuarican), for believing in me; for letting me proof read to you over and over again, for helping me rise above my inner doubts; for being so patient and understanding; for bringing me a hot cup of tea as I continued to write late night; for helping me with my daughters while I worked on this dream; for putting a smile on my face whenever I had to relive a sad moment while editing my poetry. Thank you from the bottom of my heart. You are a unique soul and it has been a blessing in my life to have met you.

Table of Contents

Maria Ester Flores
(La Grilla)

As much as I love to write and through my writing express my true feelings regarding any situation in my life, when it comes to my aunt, it is automatic writers block (my heart never said goodbye), the instant tears always cloud my thoughts, and the pain is unbearable. It is easier to just hold on to our last happy moments together. As far as I'm concerned she is still part of every step I take and worthy of the very first page in my book.

When you are doing well in life so many are willing to surround themselves with your presence, but when you are down and out, mentally lost, broke or in a dark place it takes a natural selfless soul to stand by your side and point out your good qualities. Numerous times she lifted my spirit. I will forever be indebted to this woman, who was not only my aunt; she was my best friend, my partner in crime, the one I trusted with my truest thoughts.

Not a day goes by without her advice being as meaningful and vital to my decision making in life as it was when she was alive. Her unique strengths and rare beautiful soul are still my inspiration (my motto) whenever I feel like giving up. I can hear her whisper in my ear (get up Betty and show up no matter what) brush it off and smile back at this cruel and judgmental world with your head held up high.

This book is a dream I shared with my aunt for many years. I miss her dearly and wish she was here to witness this accomplishment. I want to believe she's smiling at me from afar. I love you, and in my screaming voice (I beat the odds titi).

Our Guardian Angel

when my world would turn upside down
and over my happy days came a big black cloud
you always knew exactly what to say or do
to turn my frown right back into a smile.

Whether it was good or bad what I had to say
You were always around to listen and make
My feelings your own; you could see in me
Even the things I had yet not told
Even in silence we would unite our thoughts
Together we were one perfect mind.

Around you all of my problems suddenly didn't matter
Together we would always end up in laughter
Filling me with strength and the sense to control my actions
To understand and respect God's plan was your last lesson.

So after making peace with my pain and
learning to live with it inside
I take it as a blessing from God to have shared with you so
many years in my life
You were so much more than an aunt;
you were my best friend
And even though you're no longer here in flesh
One thing remains real only now like my guardian angel
You are still behind me one hundred percent.

A Mother's Love
(for young mothers)

when you become a mother at a very young age (especially growing up the way I did), even though you're forced to grow up fast pace, it doesn't change your age. You are literally a kid trying to raise another kid to the best of your ability. You can only make decisions based on your knowledge, and if you don't have an adult around to guide you in a positive way along with real authority, you learn by making mistake after mistake. You are stuck juggling what you define as responsibilities while having fun and naturally reacting your age. You grow up alongside your children almost as siblings. I knew about making money and I knew I'd climb any mountain to give them everything I was deprived of as a child, but I now know there was so much more involved. I am not trying to make excuses for myself and this doesn't minimize in any way how much I love my daughters; I'm expressing myself as the voice for all young mothers around trying to make it without any real guidance. Those of us who have been there and done that I feel have a duty to advise them, embrace them and teach them what we now know due to experiences. Being on another level in your life doesn't give you the right to judge the younger generation or gossip about them forgetting at one point in your life you may have been as ignorant or worse. Women should be helping one another. If you see someone else's child doing something wrong or making bad decisions, instead of gossiping about them, how about you do your part and speak to their parent, be proactive in positively shaping the future by how we give back to the younger generation. We already have enough against us trying to protect our children from the streets, media, teen suicide, peer pressure, insecurities, ect. Please take the time to honestly ponder on these humble thoughts, and I hope you find it in your heart to be part of making a difference one day at a time, one child at a time.

A Mother's Mission

You are like looking in the mirror with an exclamation mark
This is why I've been so over protective while watching you
grow up.
I was full of goals and dreams as a child too, but
They were taken from me and I don't want the same
happening to you.
In my teen years I also dared to create my own rules
Now I wish there would have been an adult around telling
me what to do.
I made so many mistakes I could never take back
I know you must make your own but life is so much easier
with a map.
You might look at me like the worse teacher to have
As you criticize the bad choices in my past, but
Have you ever wondered if those are my reasons?
While making the decision to follow you like a shadow to
the end
I'm truly sorry if you felt trapped
I don't want to control your every step
I just want to be the crutch you hold until you're strong
enough to stand alone.
You must feel like your plans are the best, yet
My best thinking as a kid developed into someone grown
full of regrets.
I'm not trying to compare our strengths or fill your mind
with fear, but
It's my job to be your second pair of eyes until you can see
clear.

Feeling Some Type of Way
(A Chameleon)

This particular section of randomly selected poems is one of my favorites. Usually I separate my poetry based on emotions, but these poems even though they are different in their own right, the energy behind them is the same. They were written to quench my inner thirst of screaming out from the depths of my soul to those trying to take advantage of a very vulnerable point in my life. Thoughts which were best kept inside then, as I tried to make sense of my undercover haters. These poems describe the fighter in me, my very prideful and cocky side; the tool and wisdom I used to rise above all. I learned to accept others for who they are (even if its ugly). I learned you can't control what other's say or do, but you do have control of your own actions. I chose to get up, stand for my beliefs, brush the undercover haters off like dust and give them even bigger reasons (in my Katt Williams voice) to feel free to hate on me. Life is what you make of it. This was my own unique way of expressing this amazing God given gift to find my creative side in the midst of any situation when, I was "feeling some type of way". So, this section is dedicated to my inner roar and of course to my own personal stack of haters.

Labelled

I may appear
Like a cold soul impossible to feel
Like a person who responds from impulse
Never taking into consideration what anyone else has been
through.
But, if you dare take more than a second to overlook the
rumors
And get to know the real me; you will see a heart working
extra hard to still
Function underneath the bruising and pump enough blood
to at least exist
Even if behind every beat, the drive is all the blows I had to
endure and swallow
Re-inventing myself hit after hit in order to force a
tomorrow
Without a clue on the ending result, just an inner rush of
pain and sorrow.
With everything to lose and unsure of what I'll gain, so my
escape
Instead of going completely insane was to fake a smile and
stand proud
Next to each and one of my decisions whether they were
right or wrong
Until my made out of bricks bubble became more believing
than
Accepting I was broken and full of rage.
Giving my new ways valid reasons to retaliate first in a just
incase attitude

I rather wipe your tears than steer away from my defensive mechanism rules
Unbreakable rules created with no room for exceptions
I rather learn another lesson from my own mistakes than to embrace the role of a victim.
I rather you think whatever you want about my outer layers as I avoid revealing
Because, if you take the time to dig deeper; you will see the fire of unbearable pain
Burning inside of a woman traumatized from different kinds of abuse and humiliations.
How does one come back from such terror? Locking it all up in a mental box
Holding on to it like some sacred treasure wrapped in a bow of pressure
As a reminder of what happened the moments she practiced humble, sweet and tender.
I may appear, like a cold soul impossible to feel, but
You have no idea the measures, the chase, the state of mind, the years of fear
What was at stake and what took place when you labeled the emotionless look on my face
I did and I am a product of the environment of my horrific past
I did and I am whatever I felt was needed for me to heal even if you don't understand.

Forever Different

I could be the same like everyone else
Wishing a change comes all by itself
Living a routine; afraid to challenge myself.

I could live a lie just like people I know
Whom for the rest of their lives
Their surroundings, is all they'll ever know
Experiencing life by what other people once told
But, I don't think about it twice when taking a risk
There's not one opportunity I'm willing to miss.

Because when I die none of it will matter
How much is in the bank or what outfit am I buried in?
My last thoughts will be my kids and all I've accomplished
Not how many times I failed, but how strong I've always
been.

I'll smile, as I take my last breath knowing I didn't go
Without testing the waters
Regardless of which decisions were right or wrong
Making sure I'm always the star of the show
A unique soul from the day I was born.

Never taking no for an answer
The mission becomes finding a loop hole
Creating the way on my own, and of course
I'm the only one who needs to understand the reasons
I love being me; forever different.

Walk In My Shoes

Whichever way I look
Someone is ready to give their input about my life
Opinions given in spite, trying to dig the knife deeper
Expressing how they've hated on me the whole time.
Some I guess have nothing better to do
Bored and disgusted of who they've become
Why else would my failures be your number one obsession?
To feel like a somewhat accomplished person; I'm flattered
Even my rock bottom is a worthy clue for success
Even on my worst day I can teach you a lesson.
For others, it's just a sneaky scheme to make a move
Hoping my depression will be your way in
If a woman in a vulnerable state is what you call smooth
I just don't give a fuck today, but
To you that's an important conversation.
And what if the rumors are true? Still, what does that
make you?
How much truth do you stand by?
Are you a complete soul when you close your eyes at night?
No, you choose to hide behind judging someone else
Instead of putting all your focus in the areas where you
need help
On levels in which I'm far beyond, and can school you on
how it's truly done.
Do you want to know my secret??
I stay humble and fun
That's what keeps me young while you follow me around
stunned
About my natural glow you envy so much.

My sympathy and heart still goes out to all
It must be very exhausting and hard not liking who you are
But, why can't I take a walk in this mood of "today, I just
don't give a fuck"
Or stop if I want to smell the roses, without you
Entertaining more gossip by acting concerned while asking
about my losses.
I can see right through the very shallow you
Your fakeness is your most visible flaw
I know your actions and thoughts like yesterday's news
If wishing I don't get back up is the highlight of your life
Even with everything I have going wrong; I feel sorry for you.
Whichever way I look
Someone is ready to give their input about my life
Opinions given in spite; trying to dig the knife deeper
As if they could walk in my shoes.

The Little Girl Inside

I'm searching for the little girl inside
To give her a hug, and tell her she's going to be alright
There are no reasons anymore for her to run and hide
Those whom hurt her are now gone
Tell her she's all grown up, and not afraid to fight.

But, I've kept her buried for so long, and
Not exactly sure in which part of my soul she resides
I'd have to start by apologizing
For all the years it took me to mentally rewind
It was easier then to pretend she had died
Than to admit who she had become while adapting to the
street life.

I would have to explain we were too young to mend her
broken heart
In order to survive in the streets your heart must be rock hard
And she was too sweet and innocent to play the part.
I will let her know we made it through it all
Even if as an adult we stand with numerous scars.

If it wasn't so important to remember who I was
I would keep her in the dark, where we have been kept
safe from
Reliving the nightmares of the way she was harmed.
I'm searching, so I can genuinely embrace who I am, and
Feel worthy of my blessings regardless of my actions to
make it this far.

I have to look her in the eyes and finally let her speak
So she can whisper into my mind how proud she is of me
For beating the odds and chasing our childhood dreams
For never allowing us to believe who other people see.

Laughing Out Loud

I laugh at those who think they have something on me
you can be erased as fast as a wink of an eye, from the
circle of my life
and I will loose no sleep.
It will seem as if we never crossed paths in each other's lives
Did we truly meet or did you just fulfill a task?
Was it meant to last or did you ignore the signs?
I laugh at those who think I've lost my mind
Maybe I chose to be wild, let go, and lose control for a while
I live in my own world, where there's no flow but mine.
Do you speak of what you know? Or were you too slow to
realize
You played the role of an old piece of gum, stuck behind
my fun
An unnoticed character of once upon a time.
I laugh at those who think they have the power to take
Did you actually gain something or were you left with my
spare change?
A puppet, acting out whatever I had planned for the day.
I laugh at those who think I'm being fooled
Because I'll entertain, benefiting from your silly games too
Because there's no reason to be afraid, I'm the one who
makes the rules.
I laugh at those who think I'll hesitate
I stand by my own actions and self-motivate
I am a rare breed; I am an unidentifiable style; I am
impossible to duplicate
I am unique, without an expiration date
I laugh at those who wish I'll go away.

Your Inner Voice

So silent yet strong are the words
Locked away in one's heart
The feelings behind them can create
Unexpected fear and unstoppable tears
Unspoken words but more real than any verse I'll ever write.
For some, it also starts to feel like a curse
Because reality puts up a fight and may steal
By forcing you to choose what sounds safe, or right
Avoiding what naturally causes you to skip a beat inside
Tormented from memorable mistakes and hurtful goodbyes
If only one's soul could speak without doubt getting in the
way and clouding our minds.
And so we live afraid to wonder what if?
Afraid to ask yourself why there's something else you wish
So the truth grows old and the tears run dry
Buried deep down where it will never be told
Beneath decisions you made; beneath politically correct
rehearsed lies
Hiding the unquenched thirst of running for your life
Leaving in the dark, locked away in one's heart to rot forever
Those inner voices heard from the start.

Poker Face

A new hand has been dealt; who's turn is it now?
Which weak back bone will I have to hold down?
This player sounds cocky but the reality is exhaustedly
profound
This player sounds like an expert but I'm just used to
playing the part
Of the one who picks up all the pieces; putting aside
whatever I need or want.

A new hand has been dealt; who's turn is it now?
Which weak back bone will I have to hold down?
What else must I put aside so that someone I love will be
able to shine?
Bypassing all of their lies and betrayals; accepting like a pro
the cards that were dealt
Replacing my pain with hope and help, even if I burn in the
process of healing
Someone I love inner hell; someone I love dreams and goals
Capable of carrying their loads and closing my eyes to my
own mission in life.

A new hand has been dealt; who's turn is it now?
Which weak back bone will I have to hold down?
I'm stuck in the shadows of the duties I swallow; choking
from the knot in my throat
Hoping they eventually let go; before this internal frown
out-weighs my poker face smile

Spreading myself thin; expected to always check in for what someone I love chose
Taking a secret deep breath, without a chance for this poker face player
One day be set free to play my own hand.

Invincible

Sometimes I wish I were invincible
So I could sit quietly and listen to my thoughts
Without them being corrupted by what others need or want.

I yearn for time of my own for the simple but meaningful details
I'd enjoy so much; like a walk alone in the park meditating
Especially in the fall watching the beautiful and colorful leaves drop.

Why must I be referred to as bitchy, when I don't want anyone around
We're not all perky and clingy; some of us just don't want to be found
What I seek no one can give me; in this journey I hope to find, myself.

Am I not allowed sacred moments, where my soul is free to jump out?
Without being asked where am I going, because my silence creates doubt
Many are invested in knowing; my choices are important to those whom I help.

Has it ever occurred to them that I may be a loner? In need of no attention
Even if I seem distant, cold or mean; my actions shouldn't be questioned
My life, my style; at least for a little while, why can't I go unnoticed?

Sometimes I wish I were invincible
So I could sit quietly and listen to my thoughts
Without them being corrupted by what others need or want.

I've Opened My Eyes

I've finally opened my eyes.
Facing reality means honestly saying goodbye.
In the beginning of such journey the paths
May seem dark and deprived, because when
You completely set all the bullshit aside
You realize who's worth keeping in your life
And most likely your circle will dramatically minimize
Which, is a blessing in disguise.

I've finally opened my eyes.
Dealing with the truth means there's no room left for
All the games and lies which used to corrupt your train of
thought
Forcing impulsive childish moves to ridiculously shine in
the hood
While others thrive off your ignorant ways
Entertained by your dirty laundry on front page.
I finally understood it's in my best interest to stay away and
focus
On never again making the same mistakes, and if confusion
ever takes place
I promise to pray while I patiently wait.

I've finally opened my eyes.
Such realization means, not allowing what other people
have to say
Define who I am no matter what; standing strong on my
own two feet

Like someone who truly knows the difference between defeat and a change of heart.
I no longer need an approval; I no longer need a partner in crime
My words are not attached to a bitter face; this is not a secret attack from pride.
I'm not equip to give advice; I don't claim to be a pro at getting pass negativity
Part of enjoying this new found tranquility, is not judging those who are still blind.
Such realization means I understand this intervention is about me
My past; my future, and present relationship with God
As for the rest; tell them I'm busy feeling empowered and grateful
For finally opening my eyes.

An Inner Roar

There's this beautiful monster asleep inside.
She resides deep down in my unspoken desires
Tired of waiting to be awaken and once again feel alive
Reliving her best moments by taking consecutive rides
Through the memories of when she was the queen of the
night
Before she was forced to retire.
There's this mountain of ashes where fire used to burn so
bright
The evidence hides behind the sparkle in her eyes
In the half smile she fights out of her soul every time
She's asked to play nice, when losing control is her style.
There's this wild untamable side missing a stage of her own
Her true inner laugh died years ago and was left
In a frozen like mode on a secret quest to find
A place where she's allowed to explode and thrive
In the mischief full of sexy evil thoughts stuck in her head
Eager to fulfill her needs of an indecent touch
Spreading her contagious disease of unnatural lust
Expressing the extremely naughty vocabulary of her
seductive threats
The right choice of words is a must; when she's free to
attack.
There's this roar I repeatedly hear so near yet, so far
A passionate storm lost at calm in an uncomfortable form
Pretending to enjoy being content while constantly sensing
a void
Bored and unsure of how long this nightmare will last.

There's this silent cry of loud, bold, young, fun taking pride in her erotic life
Disguised into a poem of a suffocated old spiritless unexciting heart
An overload of past experiences tied into a knot, reduced to remember or write
There's this beautiful monster asleep inside.

Falling in Love
(Lust)

Every single girl in the world, regardless of race, age, financial bracket or upbringing, dreams about the day when she finally falls in love. You get butterflies in your stomach; you start daydreaming about all the possibilities, in your mind you guys have been in an entire relationship before you actually exchange words. A woman knows from the moment she sets eyes on him whether or not he has a chance, the rest is just a matter of time. This feeling called love has the power to drive you insane. Even as you are consciously making these out of control impulsive decisions, the actual feeling along with your actions are unexplainable. Love is like the air we breathe; we can't see it nor touch it, but we feel it. I included the word lust as part of my title for this section of emotions, because it is also an uncontrollable situation which feels awesome. They are two type of feelings which are literally inseparable. Only when you have truly overcome a relationship, can you have the ability to separate the two and identify which category you were realistically involved in. Either way, both feelings are something to experience, if you're so lucky. However, these feelings don't ask for permission, they don't knock; they walk right into your life and simply take over. Most of us, at least once, have looked at an ex and wondered "what the hell was I thinking?" but, when in the moment, you'll be surprised who you could fall in love with, or lust. There are so many levels and a lot of baggage that comes with such feelings, both positive and negative, but these emotions focuses on when and how it all first started, or when you are right smack in the middle. There are no instructions, it can happen anywhere, with anyone and you will go against anything and everyone in the name of love, or lust. We all go through it, so women please stop judging and gossiping, putting each other down instead of understanding we have all been there, have you ever lifted a stranger's spirit?

Unexplainable Love

The way you love your parents
Is perfectly understood
The way you love your siblings
Is all you know that's true

Growing up
The rest of your family and close friends
Have been there since you can remember
So it's natural for you to love them

But when another soul plants a seed
In the middle of your heart
And you lose control of your beliefs
Of your feelings; of your decisions
Of when it's time to let go
You realize there's another type of love
Not talked about at home

Love for a stranger
Becoming someone you can't live without
Even if loving him could put you in danger
Your feelings will make sure you keep him around

And while this is all going down
Your heart wonders why, when and how?
You could hardly know someone
Fall blindly in love, and forget about yourself.

Curiosity

The curiosity is driving me nuts
It's a battle inside every time we talk
Cautiously selected words
General and innocent
Yet, my eyes I'm sure tell him different.

It's becoming an overwhelming mission
To maintain space between us
He might be what I'm missing
My heart says, my body listens
But my mind explains he's young and ignorant.

I must keep these thoughts hidden along with the glow
In my eyes whenever he shows up, I get so hot
He's an adrenaline rush which blows my all into pieces
Leaving me puzzled of why not ignore reason.

It gets harder each day to zip my mouth shut and act
surprised
Like I don't know what he's thinking or
Why he continuously comes by.

Lust struck turning this battle uncontrollably exciting every
time
But it's my responsibility as the adult
Even if the curiosity is driving me nuts
To, write down these thoughts without getting out of line.

On The Hush

I made it my business to touch private property.
I don't like the fact that we have to hide, but
I'll take my chances as long as the prize, is
Having him by my side when I'm feeling naughty.
There's something about the way he touches me.
Worth breaking all the rules in the book
Replaced the definition of decency with extreme seduction
I don't care if I'm the substitution or an illusion
Everyone has the rights to pick their own poison, and
There's something about the way he rubs his hands
All over my body like lotion.
I'm not in a state of confusion
I get it; he's not mine, well, at least not for the moment
I didn't lie to get him in bed; I'm not heartless or blind
We don't pretend like this is going to last
We are just enjoying what we shouldn't have
There's something about the way he says my name
As he's licking down my back.
I never asked for permission to sleep with this man
Remorse doesn't know how to hide; I'd lie to claim regret
So I won't apologize or take the fault for this disrespect
In the end it was his decision to fulfill this experience
He's the one who will have to explain, if we were ever caught
There's something about the way he pleads for another night
He makes it his business to keep us on the hush.
No need to question his other life; his reasons why
My mind honestly is at peace; in me guilt does not reside
No one has the power to lead who doesn't want to be led on
Obviously something wasn't right; if he chose to do wrong

Or not, but then again; we don't meet up for the details
Just because I don't want this to stop doesn't mean
I don't understand we are only two lonely friends
I stick to the facts; the mere thought of him gets me wet
The explosion of our lust when kisses become bites
There's something about the way, he excites my insides.

Like Butter I Melt

I don't know what to do, to get my mind off of you.
I'm stuck in the middle of the lies and my truth
Especially when you give me that certain look
The fire in your eyes take over whatever pride I had left
Forgetting the reasons why I came here so upset
Focusing my feelings only on the exact moment in time
Ignoring the harsh reality of you not being really mine.
Blinded by the way you replace your hands with your tongue
These moments become more powerful than any of my
realistic thoughts.
I walked in your room with my mind made up
Hoping to stay strong and stand by my pride
But your words mellow me down; your touch is so profound
The sounds you make is music to my ears
I risk my heart every day just to keep you near.
Your body heat tests how bad I want to set me free
I came here full of strength to get my things and leave
Yet, I'm naked again, underneath your sheets.
I don't know what to do, to get my mind off of you
I'm stuck in the middle of the lies and my truth
And I'm in need of some serious help
Because, around this man like butter I melt.

Lusting in Silence

It's incredible how eye contact works
Without any words I knew he'd walk out first
And I will say my goodbyes to the crowd
Giving him enough time to turn his car around
So we can meet down the street
Headed towards a hotel
Where we can finally express ourselves
Where our thoughts can run wild and free
The silence remains intense
Rushing to rent a room
Ignoring phone calls from our mutual friends
Our hearts and minds understand
We will communicate between sheets
Covered in a lot of sweat
No need to ask as we fall sleep
Our reasons why, are best unsaid
We're both content with the gradual growth
Unnecessary pressure will hurt the flow
Our lips let's us know it's worth the risk
I've been silently lusting over this kiss
Secretly written poems; wanting more
Anxious for the next unspoken hint
It's incredible I tell you how eye contact works
Words replaced by suspense
Since the day two friends, decided to flirt.

Lust Slash Love

I walked into the room
Knowing what we were there to do.
Now, the teasing him for a while is over
The seductive smile interrupted by the crowd
The hints accompanied by a wink without action
The curiosity of forbidden satisfaction.
The reading between the lines conversations
Leading to an undercover sexual investigation
Staying up all night writing expressing
The very intense inspiration
Caused by the look in your eyes
As you asked the right questions.
Yet, I continuously kept you guessing
Adding fire to the already heated communication.
Thoughts, desires and wild expectations
It was a dream with realistic limitations.
Until my reality changed leaving me a single person
Giving us the option to escape with no hesitation.
I'm in the bathroom afraid of my own intentions
Wondering if he's another mistake I'm making.
He's so young knocking on the door wanting to enter
The music is on and the bed is waiting for
Everything that while drinking we mentioned.
He yelled "the blunt is rolled and I turned off our phones"
Reminding me with the very demanding manly tone of voice
I had been physically and emotionally alone for way too long.
So, I figured "what the heck" and turned the knob
I walked into the room
Knowing what we were there to do
But never imagined I would fall in love too.

He Stole My Heart

I've been at war with myself from day one, about us
Fighting to take back my heart.
I walked off that first night, feeling so seductive and strong
And now, I feel so sad and weak whenever he is gone.
My pride and rage comes up with different ways to let him go
I can't explain this hold he has over my mind and soul
Every minute of my day is spent thinking of him
Face to face my wall crumbles; my pride stumbles
Humbly forcing me into accepting
My feelings for him are out of control.
It's hard to believe how quickly he stole the invincible key
To walk in and out of my life as he pleases
I've been known to be harsh, cold and mean
Especially when my intelligence is being insulted
Yet, I'll willingly play the role of stupidity
Surrendering to the lies just to watch him sleep.
Weeks ago I was sure I'd have a little fun
And eventually get bored, but I was instantly swept off my feet.
He is intensively becoming the most important thing in my world
I think I've been put under a spell, because
I've become his property and everyone labeled me as his girl.
My actions tell me it's too late to send him to hell
As jealousy takes over regardless of any embarrassing moment
More afraid of how I'll react if I were to see him with someone else.
This is driving me crazy; second guessing everything

While trying to mentally figure him out
Why can't I shake this obvious obsession?
I'm in love with the thief and the army of me, doesn't
know where to start?
I've been at war with myself from day one, about us
Fighting to take back my heart.

Ghetto Love

In the midst of a full moon
And not another soul on the block
On the corner of Chesnut St. and Monroe
Two free spirits dared to kiss on the hush.
He fearlessly grabbed a hold of her face
This time she's not his connect
But the girl he's always dreamed about and known.
Hoping by catching her alone; he wouldn't be pushed away
For the sake of their relationship in sales
In defense of her name in the streets and flow.
So she looked both ways before rising on her tippy toes
To embrace a very dangerous yet exciting moment
They had been secretly waiting for their lips to finally lock
With their pockets full of rocks and the noise of the sirens
getting closer.
An everlasting rush for these two thugs out in the open
The amount of cops didn't stop them from physically exposing
The uncontrollable desire of when a lion demands what he
wants, or
When the untamable wicked witch from the west, casts a
spell on her sexy mark.
They unfolded unexplored magic, extra sensitive and naked
to their every touch
A historic explosion happened of unspoken passion and
intense lust.
A tornado awakening a volcano and after centuries of only
imagining, it erupts
Ignoring the line they were crossing and consequences if
they were caught

Unraveling their fantasy became what was most important.
In the midst of a full moon and not another soul on the block
There was a different kind of transaction
This time they were exchanging a new level of trust.
There was no money, rocks, games or fame involved
Just an everlasting rush for these two thugs out in the open
On the corner of Chesnut St. and Monroe
Two free spirits dared to kiss on the hush
Baring witness to the birth of their ghetto love.

Do You Know

Do you know what you've done?
You've put a smile on the face
Of a woman who walks around with a broken heart.

A woman who lives out her days, but
Alone in the dark are her thoughts.

It's all about the math, and the responsibilities she has
To others it might seem different on the block
But once she's home
She's a mother, a daughter, a sister and a friend
Yet, she feels so alone
She's a woman in a relationship where the man is always
gone.

For them, she does more than she should
And she's always misunderstood.

Do you know what you've done?
You've put a smile on the face
Of a woman who walks around with a broken heart.

On Fire

I closed my eyes
Mesmerized by the feeling of his tongue
Licking all over my neck and spreading my legs softly
Teasing with his every touch as I'm being undressed
There's a million thoughts running through my head
But, before I had a chance to suggest maybe we should stop
I was completely naked on the bed with my fantasy man
on top.

I closed my eyes again
Embarrassed by the speed of my shaking thighs
This young man is making all the right moves
Accurate when he hits a spot; my bottom is all wet
His saliva mixed with cum; toes curled up
I can't believe how much I continuously bust
Hitting all types of high notes
This kid is on fire, and the night has just begun
My body gladly surrendered to his flow.

I peaked quickly one more time
I needed to see; I was on number three, and he hadn't
broken a sweat
Decided I might as well let go, enjoy, and relax
It is going to be a problem getting up from this bed
I escaped for a night of fun, but this beating I didn't expect
To have my back blown out; to fall in love with his sex
For now, it's best I keep my eyes closed.

Head Over Heels

They say it's wrong I've been by his side this long
By now our names should be engraved in their tongues
They explain their reasons why I must move on
Not caring their words are hurting me so much.

They're talking about the one who holds my heart
And expect me to keep my mouth shut.

Should I pretend to agree just so they'll leave me alone?
Haven't they ever felt something so strong?
When all the obstacles in the world are not enough
To lose touch or walk away from, even if they think I'm nuts!

They can judge me and gossip all they want
I'll still defend until the end our love
There's nothing no one can do to get in the middle of us
I'm head over heels in love.

Love at First Sight

For me, the meaning of love had become a challenge
Capturing the look of true interest in his eyes
Super conceited and full of pride as I glance at a guy
Indulging in my seductive side were the real motives
Holding his heart in my hand like a trophy I had won
Maybe because of all the pain I secretly held inside
From putting my guard down more than once.
Except this time; I couldn't execute my Oscar winning lines
His natural spark jump started my heart
The truth behind his innocent smile didn't allow me
To play around with the moment or wisely choose my words
I found myself speechless, nervous and shy.
His realness and sweetness paralyzed the wickedness
Instantly erasing the darkness which had taken over my life
Just when I planned to never again fall for anyone
I was reminded of the power of love at first sight
It doesn't knock at your door or calls to make sure
Before it stops by to rearrange your feelings and thoughts.
Two humans can spiritually touch each other's souls
With one look, one smile and a simple hello.

Love Hurts
(We live, love and learn)

women are the strongest and most beautiful creatures created by God. We bring fourth new life (sounds magical) and it is, except such a task also comes with gaining an enormous amount of weight, mood swings, stretch marks, pain and wait; not to mention going through this self-sacrifice is also a decision based on falling in love and believing that man when he tells you he loves you and will remain by your side until the end. Yet, most of us end up raising our children alone. We have no choice but to step up to the plate, and boy does it hurt trying to figure out how is it so easy for him to walk away? We start questioning everything we were programmed to believe regarding true love through romantic movies growing up, and books where there was always a happy ending. We are raised with these high expectations and then forced to suffer the extremely painful reality when love hurts (literally). Women are the masters of multi-tasking; from taking care of their children, working, cooking, cleaning and the list goes on. We should get a medal and we should be pampered every night before going to sleep, because women genuinely love and care for others and it goes unnoticed, and unappreciated. We take pride in all we do and when we fall in love (without any instructions) we are naturally prepared to give our all. Unfortunately, this is only half our story, attached to the list is also heartache, pain, betrayal, lies, tears and hopefully for our sake, forgiveness, but we never forget, do we? A woman with a broken heart is very dangerous. We may act like fools while in love but when love becomes anger, we add to the list revenge. Society likes to point the finger at bitter women lashing out in rage as a form of self-defense. Behind every mad or bitter woman there's a story to tell of a no good man who damaged a once very fragile and beautiful heart. I'm not afraid to talk about the different emotions. The rollercoaster we call love and life. We live, we hurt, we learn and some of us write. If you are able to identify with my poems in this section (I can't stress it enough) please stop fighting each other, be good to one another realizing and respecting all women go through the same emotions throughout their lives. The power of words can be both amazing and dreadful; the woman you are gossiping about may be in pain and instead of helping some no good man or society drag her through the mud, how about you help lift her spirit? My advice to women is: the greatest love of all aside from loving God, is when you learn to truly love yourself and know your worth, so when the right one does come along you don't make him pay for someone else's mistakes. Pay close attention to his actions not his words, because his actions will define whether or not he's worthy of all you have to offer, and last but not least; once you've found the one don't forget to include God in the equation, because without prayer it's impossible for true love to conquer and rise above all the temptations and evil envious people in this cruel world.

The Need to Belong

When loneliness is all you've known
A liar can sweep you off your feet and lift your soul.

When your surroundings have always been cold
A sweet lie can warm up your insides.

When everyone else left you alone with a broken heart
Your heart will unconsciously trust
The one who sticks around even if it's just to fight.

When you've been abused for so long
A soft touch after a bruise seems thoughtful and polite.

When you were never taught real love
A frog can say those magical three words
Women long for so much, and a dirty pond you'll call home
Giving your all blinded by the need to belong.

The Reality of Love

I'm really starting to hate
This feeling called love
It drives you to do things in life
That you don't need, you just want.
No matter what you're going to cry
You think you're so tough until you realize
"Shit" I'm in love
and regardless of the amount of tears
coming down from your eyes
your heart is begging you, telling you
you will miss your other half at the end of the night.
You start to forgive what you know is not right
Anything to avoid the pain
Of your loved one walking away
Either way you remain stressed out
Love hides the difference between real and fake
And all of a sudden you're afraid to be alone again
That feeling called love is not your friend.
Whoever told you this; lied
You get no clues on how to heal
You grow up waiting for your turn to love
And it's only after "shit" I'm in love
That the rest reveals.

She Who Laughs Last Laughs Best

You laughed when I asked you to leave
So sure I'd be calling you soon
With an excuse of why you should come back.
I imagine as the days went by
You grew confusedly mad at the fact
That those words had been my last.
Our story took a turn for the best
And now it's you who feels alone and hurt
I hope you're beginning to learn and understand
How cold and cruel you were.
Molding such a beautiful and warm heart
Into a broken soul afraid to love again
So confident I'd never outgrow what we once had.
Though I will admit as you were leaving
I didn't know if I was strong enough to stand by my decision
But every day my decision became more believing
better than the crazy way we were living.
I heard you were drunk yelling "she's the one"
To anyone who would listen
Did you mention you crushed all the love I had?
Did you mention you had fun watching me emotionally
collapse?
Begging you every day for years to change the way you'd act
Yet, you showed no mercy, so I will show no regrets
She who laughs last laughs best.

Now It's My Turn

You said: you hate me now more than ever
You said: you will never look at me the same
Yet, you're still standing there
I hope you're not waiting for me to cry or explain.
I will not change my decision
Just like you wouldn't change your ways
Are you hoping I seduce you to stay?
Probably, since back in the day
I would sugar coat my feelings
Based on the sad expression on your face, but not today
You took my kindness for weakness
And always avoided discussing my reasons
Now, I have nothing else to say.
Another man is fulfilling what I was missing
Healing all the pain you gave
So the longer it takes for you to walk out
The longer I'll enjoy watching you drown in your shame.
The entire neighborhood knows you've been replaced
How does it feel to be on front page?
How does it feel to be the one trying to escape the rumors?
Is it driving you insane to get a taste of your own doings?
Don't bring up the love you ruined for so long
Don't delay walking out the door
You should be an expert at walking away
You should be an expert at moving on.

Taken for Granted

Did you really think I wasn't aware?
I walked in first to take a deep breath and brush off the psychotic urge
Of literally chopping off your head as I noticed the stare.
Would it be fair to let you know?
As you supposedly returned to the car to get your coat, and
Probably pass her a note; one of your friends confessed
If given the chance I would never be left alone.
He ordered my breakfast and knew exactly how I like my eggs
Asked me if I was content with the chosen table and pulled the chair out
For me before I sat; continuing his conversation by saying how I deserve the best.
Unlike you, I know my place until the day I decide to let you go
However, his sweet words and effort can make any woman wonder
Should it be that easy to give someone else your number?
Should I give you a dose of your own game?
And take over your amateur ways when playing the role of an undercover lover.
Should I make up an excuse of needing space so I too can escape?
And experience what it feels like when someone truly interested
Actually plans for you a real and exciting date?
Should I let this anger gain control?
And become the reason why I allow another man to drive me home?

My thoughts as I watched your breakfast getting cold
My thoughts as you apologized for the delay without your coat.
Do you really think I'm that dumb?
Your rebuttals are lame and your games, so old.
Keep thinking you sound believing taking my love for granted
Wandering off with other women leaving me up for grabbing
Willing to risk breaking my heart for a few minutes of sexist satisfaction
It won't be long before I put my own thoughts and feelings into actions.

The Better Person

I chose to be the better person
I'm sure you saw it in my face expression
How hard it was to pull myself together
The love in me anxious to fight for what I believe
A broken heart in need of answers
Some way, some how
I was able to turn around without saying goodbye
Every step I took left behind pieces of all I knew
My thoughts and memories are in shock
You said it would always be just us
Now someone else will sleep with you at night
I could rip her apart
But, what will I gain by hurting her in the end
Nothing will ever change the fact that she slept with my man
You will become a hero among your friends
And I'll be the one stuck; forced to pretend
I can really forgive a betrayal to this extend
Walking away I'll save my sanity and eventually mend
A wound you will never erase or understand
So let it be God who teaches you a lesson
I chose to be the better person.

Blinded

I covered every one of his mistakes
Telling myself his actions were just a phase.
Never once questioned when he came home late
Focused on making sure I pleased him in every way.
Ignoring the expressions on his face as he lied
Telling myself when the phone rang late at night
He left because making money was his drive.
He even went as far as asking me to be his wife
And my eyes shined full of excitement
Forgetting the necessary ties
Like the ring, trust, loyalty and respect
Qualities which should have been expressed by both sides
Instead, of me continuously swallowing the
embarrassments.
I should have dropped him like a bad habit then
Yet, I went above and beyond to help him rise
Allowed him to feel like a man
Though, everything we have is mine.
I figured as long as he hid to do his dirt
He wouldn't need to deny and I wouldn't have to hurt
Until he publicly stepped out of line
Forcing me to regroup and rescue my pride.
First, I took a trip to the stash
Second, I put the couple of things he had when we met;
outside
With a note letting him know he had broken my heart, but
At least I was no longer blind and finally free to eventually
heal
I wished him luck on his journey without a dime.

Third, I promised myself to never again
Allow someone else's theory of love cloud my mind
To know my worth so I can always walk with my head up high
Whether I'm walking alone or with someone by my side.
Woman's intuition will warn you that something is not right
So don't insanely cover up while he sucks your heart dry
The outcome will be the same whether you decide to say
goodbye today
Or take that important step in your life, ten years down the
line.
The pain you're so afraid to embrace may be a blessing in
disguise.

My Bitter Sweet Revenge

You will suffer my pain
Even if I grow old and gray with this revenge
This is what I feel you deserve
And I don't want to leave this earth until you get
At least half of what you've earned
For destroying the beautiful heart, I used to have.
I refuse to take this to the grave
And I've never been one to look away
You've worked my last nerve
Creating an enormous urge to give back
The same exact treatment or worse
Hoping then I might be able to relax.
Behind every single word
There's years of planning this attack
I'll admit you were good
But, I will show you the very best
This calm bitter sweet smile on my face, you'll never forget
You started an evil game that now I want to extend.
No mercy, no remorse and of course no regrets
Don't try to bend my rules and take it like a man
It's only fair I share with you all my stress
Using specific moves to get deep into your head.
Now you know the real reasons why I remained by your side
I was never weak or blind; it just wasn't over yet
By the time I'm done with you
You will wish you never laid eyes on the wicked witch from
the west.
Witnessing your internal death is when I'll allow our goodbye
I warned you from the day you said your first lie

I asked you to seriously analyze in which part of me you'd like to invest
I told you once I had fallen in love I could be your best friend
I also warned you that a hurt me could be
The evilest person you have ever met
You will suffer my pain
Even if I grow old and gray with this revenge.

Where Did the Real Men Go?

I closed my eyes trusting every word he said
I never peaked; I never questioned, instead
I found myself in foreign lands
Allowing a man to feel like a man and lead for a change
Trying something different; looking to make amends
With how dominant I've been in the past
And how quick I can be to push anyone away
Wo dares go against my plans.
I ran with this dream of together always finding a way
Excited about finally being able to quietly rest
On a man's chest, without having to investigate everything
he says.
I promised to lay low and show some respect for the
one I chose
And in return he promised I would never have to carry
The load alone again, or stress supervising his every step.
I know nothing comes easy, so I kept busy building "it's
who I am"
Not stepping on his toes and owning up to my part of the
bargain
Starting fresh; finally relaxing and giving him a fair chance
Even if it meant accepting the role of second in command.
I thought things were slowly but surely moving along
Until I opened my eyes one day and noticed something
was wrong
I peaked; I questioned; no response, instead
I saw my world falling apart and the only promise he kept
Was to fill me up with cum while he swept our debt under
the rug.

Forcing me once again to be the rock and the carpenter
Not that this is a strange road but now I'm driving in a rush
When I'm used to watching my investments grow
Like the independent woman I am
All because for a change I did not want to budget alone.
I feel betrayed, unprotected and vulnerable in the name of
love
Now I understand why there are so many beautiful women
around
With their skin so warm and soft but their minds, hearts
and souls
So cold; a brick wall; traumatized by loss, and it shows
By the amount of fatherless children
Where did the real men go?

If I Could Only Tell My Boys

I sit here on exhaustion mode
Watching you roam the house
Waiting for me to fold and once again figure out
How we will make it through this new rough road?
Hoping I don't explode and fight about
The fact that you won't move a muscle
Leaving it always up to me; to hustle and make ends meet
When, I didn't create this family alone.
So confident I will make sure we meet our needs
Plus, a little extra so you're not so bored
In the meantime, our boys view me as the mean one
Because, I'm hardly ever home.
You get to feed them and be this great dad
They are too young to know daddy pretty much
Holds them back from the opportunity to grow and
experience
What it's like to have a normal life.
If mommy could smile more and not isolate in her room
So the tears in her eyes continue unnoticed
Staring at the multiples final notices
Worrying about the rent, food, gas, cable, light and phone
Trying not to regret the relationship she chose
Trying to understand daddy's reasons for not lending a hand
Swallowing the load; the pressure; the stress
Without being able to tell her boys.

I'm Signing the Papers

Your actions don't surprise me at all
If anything I'm mad at myself for sharing my love
And investing so much into someone whose intentions
Were always to watch me fall, only because
You were never creative enough to stand tall on your own.
Still using the same methods of survival, I see
Taking from the next in order for you to grow and succeed
Unlike back then, not one tear drop will fall from my eyes
So don't hold your breath waiting on a phone call or text
I'm signing the papers with a smile, because
Since you walked out I've been experiencing life without
stress.
I will remain smiling beyond your evil plans
Understanding obviously, you're a miserable man
Why else would you spend your precious time?
Trying to dig the knife deeper if you're the one who forced
this goodbye.
As soon as I realized my heart was stuck holding on
For unrealistic reasons since you can't miss what you didn't
actually have
I played every existing foolish role wishing we would last
Proving to myself I'm better off alone than
Wasting my energy on a miserable fuck without any real
dreams or goals.
Today, sympathy is all I feel for a divorce thirty something
year old
Making minimum wage with child support up his ass
It was cheaper to keep her but I'm so glad
You and all your unreliable ways are part of my past.

I honestly thank you for walking away and forcing me to let go
I only tried to be your friend to show our kids
They still have both their mom and dad
Is it jealousy? Is it vengeance? I don't know
But, your actions are not hurtful; it's embarrassing and I'm getting mad
Should I retaliate or continue to laugh?
Either way I'm signing the papers
No need to be false in court with the responsible and worried father act
Not having you means our bills get paid
If you want to really make sure your kids are okay and well fed
How about working on not asking me for a cent
Before I forward your new girlfriend these messages.

Someday

Someday
You will pay for all my tears
And it will be worse on you
Because in just one day
You will feel the pain I felt for years.

To hear my name
Will become your greatest fear
I will come up in your dreams
And you will need me since morning
To everyone eventually
It will get boring
When you question them on
Where I've been or where am I going?

You will weep alone
Trying to control the urge
To pick up your phone and dial my number
Just to listen to my voice.

Yes, in due time
You will have sleepless nights
Understanding the reasons why
I tried and tried.

You will be full of regrets
But by then
My efforts will be part of your past
Along with what I'm writing now.

Someday
My smile will mean your frown
And I won't have time to even look back
I'll be too busy starting fresh.

Today

Today you are ready to compromise
Today you're ready to put your ego aside, and
Look at the word unity with different eyes.

Today you're willing to erase your theory on men's rights
Today you ask me to see pass your past mistakes
Today you want me to believe our break up made a change
In your definition of how much a woman should take
Just to keep the relationship alive.

Today you are willing to step down from your inner pedestal
And invest all your energy into creating a smile where
You once left an endless frown
Today your mission is to nurture the heart
You crushed a thousand plus times.

Today you claim to have what I need to feel true happiness
inside
Please forgive the smirk on my face and the delay
For a response, but, my heart waited patiently for today
And there were moments when I thought
This day would never come.

The day you'd honestly feel some type of regret
For causing me so much pain
Maybe you have changed, and that's cool, but
Don't wonder why I refused to ever again stand by your side
Your plea is an insult to the only memories of us
When you enjoyed your life, while all I did was cry.

All Thoughts About Us

All thoughts about us
Hold me back from moving on.

The good thoughts keep me missing you so much
The bad thoughts remind me your heart can be broken
more than once.

The good thoughts tell me at least they were real feelings
from the start
The bad thoughts tell me the ending was only a percentage
of the worse part.

The good thoughts excite me enough to maybe try again
and one day give another a chance
The bad thoughts traumatize me and warns my heart to
always stay focused on the facts.

The good thoughts prohibit me from dwelling on our past
mistakes
The bad thoughts are my only proof left of all the lies,
abuse and disrespect
Of the internal wounds and wasted time I'll never get back.

Both sides weigh very heavy on my mind; there's such a
thin line between love and hate
All thoughts about us hold me back from moving on
either way.

I Moved On

I took a deep breath; nervous about how you'd react
Hoping that along with my silence
I'd be able to hold my tears back.
I'm proud of finally taking this step, and
Finding closure in a very hurtful part of my past
But, as your chest grew bigger and your voice sounded
deeper
Trying to make sense of it all; your heart was forced to feel
The honesty and realness of my thoughts, regrets,
accepting my faults
And the painful memories I'm willing to forgive but not
forget.
The difference between who I was then and who I am now
I almost found myself neglecting my needs once again
Just so you can smile and I could block the black cloud
Instantly hovering over the soul of a man who had been
shot down.
By the innocent, yet, deadly words that traveled from my
mouth
To your ears along with my silence, so my inner being could
hear
Your lungs fighting the knot in your throat to gasp for air
As your gut spoke and called my growth unfair.
I ignored my first reaction to shout defending something I had
Made clear and no longer requires your full understanding.
Instead, I open mindedly felt sympathy of the fear shinning
through
The sadness in your eyes; glowing from the flames of an
old love that

Manifested inside as a self-grudge stuck on feelings you
repeatedly crushed.
I respect the courage and awareness behind your next
move after listening
To my side; the strength it must have taken for you to drop
to the floor
On your knees proving sincerity with an apology I wasn't
waiting for
It did come as a surprise, but it doesn't save what was lost
and my tears
Are not a sign of hope; my silence is not revenge or an
opportunity to gloat
That old love you expected to find; it's just not here
anymore.
I'm proud of finally taking this step and I thank you for a
goodbye
Without us having to go to war.

Spreading Our Wings

We grew up and now there's not much we have in common
At one point I'm sure we felt love for each other
By now you're like family but more like an annoying brother.

We smile and only agree when it's time to go to sleep
Hugging one another at night, not as affection but routine
We might even sneak in a few minutes of relief
That's all it takes when you're programed to assist like a machine.

It's no mystery once morning arrives
Which one of us will be the first to pick a fight
We push those buttons until we've both stepped out of line
Anything for an excuse to leave.

We used to joke about this lie when we were younger
Getting older just reminds us of all the time we've lost
Our life is an endless war of not having the guts to say goodbye
Afraid to let go of the security blanket we knitted to stay strong.

Tears are coming down as I realize how wrong we've been
Holding on selfishly while secretly wishing to explore
We rather point the finger when there's nothing to forgive
Two rebellious teenagers hitched.

Let's understand we've naturally grown apart
Let's promise to always keep in touch
Let's decide like two mature adults, to spread our wings.

A True Connection

Communication is key
You never forget those first few words
With the one you hope becomes your king.
Understanding is a must
So other than sharing your deepest thoughts
Throughout your talk it's important you both agree
Whether or not, you also share the same goals and dreams.
It's not so much about finding out where he came from
It's more about finding out where he wants to be
Does it make sense to go on a date again?
Lust can ruin a friendship if either party becomes selfish
Over a spur of the moment decision made by the flesh
Allowing someone to treat you like a piece of meat
Listening to an interesting journey doesn't mean
He'll be the one who fulfills your real needs.
The conclusion of eventually going steady with someone
Is the impression you should give from the start
If by mentioning this, he puts up an invincible wall
Your feelings and thoughts are not respected at all
Hearing and actually listening are two very different things
Just like there's a difference between a date and being
prepped with drinks.
Does he really want to know how to become a part of your
life?
Or is he patiently waiting for the part when loneliness and
liquor takes control?
Hoping you're in a vulnerable or drunk state of mind
Watch out for the pro whose fishing for the women with a
broken heart

Take your time protecting your body and soul
Who you are and all you hold inside
Making sure both hearts are completely ready to unleash
Making sure he wants more than just the outer beauty he sees
Spoken feelings, jokes, a cute smile, an exciting night is only half the test
Know your worth; dinner doesn't pay for a kiss goodnight or a booty call at 2am
Make him work and deserve before you decide to reveal the rest
You are so much more than a few phone calls or text.
Those honest conversations are like reviewing applications
Until you've found a true connection.

Pain & Depression
(Our biggest inner battles)

Editing your own poetry means you've built up the courage to share these different emotions, however, it doesn't lessen the risk of making yourself vulnerable to relive those moments again, inside. I couldn't have chosen a better title for this book, because I held nothing back from my readers. My poems are as real as me sitting alone in tears pouring my heart out into my journal. Giving the world access to my heart is like walking into a room full of people, naked. Other than achieving my childhood dream, most importantly I've revealed so much as a form of self-therapy; the best reward will be helping those who identify with my pain. There are many levels of pain and I've endured most.

For years, I couldn't grasp the life threaten consequences of going through a massive melt down. My motto had always been to shove any feelings inside the brick wall built around my heart as a defense mechanism, and anything less than, I viewed as signs of weakness; unrealistic expectations of self forgetting I'm only human. In my culture, it's engraved in your mind not to discuss anything going on in your personal life and so you continue to shove until you eventually explode. There's but so much a human being can take and regardless of how strong-minded you consider yourself to be; a truly smart individual will ask for help when needed (life is too hard and short to be carrying the weight alone). Choose wisely who you open up to, but please take depression seriously. Pain, betrayal, setbacks and everything else will have you drowning in your own committee of thoughts, sadness and self-doubt; get a second opinion from someone you trust before making drastic decisions. Your present life and future goals depend on how well you take care of yourself internally. What is the point in smiling for the camera or lying on face book about a supposed wonderful life, while your reality is dark and ugly? The best piece of advice my father gave me was to live my reality no matter what it is and start from there.

For too long, pain, depression, rage and vengeance were my middle names. We have all been through times when we felt alone and defeated; betrayed by someone we love. It would drive me insane trying to understand, why? If I gave my all, why did they wait their turn to kick me while I was down? Why did they turn their backs when I mostly needed them? But, worst of all was losing self; those are life changing moments for better or worse, depending on the choices you make. Going through pain or being let down is inevitable, however, you don't have to be the victim. Hitting rock bottom opened my eyes, giving me a real understanding of the type of people I should surround myself with and better yet, it gave me a real understanding of the type of life I want to live. Today, with a genuine smile on my face I'm grateful to God for finding my purpose and grateful to those who wrote me off; my comeback wouldn't have been so powerful without them, as I rose above my pain and depression. Focus on you, on learning what it truly means to love yourself first and use the pain, betrayals and everyone of your hurtful experiences to bring forth the best version of you.

Mirrors to Our Soul

It is impossible to disguise
The truth behind these hazel eyes
Dark bags under them from sleepless nights
Strained pupils due to exhaustion
Wondering how they still have the ability to cry?

Feels like I've been stuck in the same emotion
Wishing they could just run dry
Even if I never truly escape the poison
why must they be so powerless to denial?
Why can't they just hold it all inside?

Words can be kept silent
Thoughts can be arrested by the mind
Yet, the heart always has a way of showing
What the body works so hard to hide.

You can demand your lips to smile
You can try and lie to those around
But, you can't pretend like you're glowing
Even if you don't make a sound.

There's this natural reaction
An inner language we can't control
The truth has unbreakable laws of it's own
Our eyes are mirrors to our soul.

Who Do I Run To?

When loneliness is taking over
But, I can't complain or show them
I'm under so much stress
Yet, it's expected of me to always
Wear the S on my chest
And hold it all together even if in the end
I'm stuck alone dealing with the mess
Of a girl who didn't ask to be in control
Part of the load is to keep a smile regardless
Disguising my inner hell and worries in style
Proving I can maintain the household in order
Without ever getting any help
But, who do I tell? Who do I run to?
Who will understand what I know of self?
How, any given day now I'm due to explode
A serious melt down from a tired soul
Being the back bone for so many; for so long
Being strong feels like a full time job
Without an incentive or a day off
Without any goals of my own to explore
Who do I run to?
When I need to have a moment
When I need to feel like I'm human
Instead of feeling like a walking solution
How come no one wonders how I'm doing?

Inside My Soul

I'm afraid to look inside my soul
I don't want to face all the pain it holds
Most of the pain is very old
By now engraved in my heart
But, if I start to mentally rewind
The bitterness might show
And I'll throw away how hard it was
All the years behind digging the hole
To bury and hide.
So, I trick my mind every day
Telling me everything is okay
Demanding I'm happy no matter what
As if the numerous falls weren't enough
To get me down
I am running on low
But, I will never let them see my frown.
I keep my pain underground
The only tears I can't stop is when I look up
Because, only God knows
Although, on the outside I seem as hard as a rock
I'm afraid to look inside my soul
Because, inside I'm torn apart.

Broken

I see the mountain
Just don't want to climb it anymore.
I've been overcoming for years
The outcome always leaves me in tears
My struggle crumbled into pieces
Worked so hard for nothing
Carried the weight with pride
They still ended up leaving
Betraying me with a bunch of lies.
I see the light
Just don't want to be guided.
In my darkness I don't have to hide
The pain of their sudden silence
Why should I continue to try?
If all this time my actions were unnoticed
And everything that took me so long to build
Within minutes they've broken.

How Come?

If smiles are free
How come they're so hard to keep?
How come for me there's always a price to pay?
Whenever I feel one on my face.

They say without laughter in your soul
You won't live to be old and gray
How come my aunt smiled every day, and
Still at a young age, six feet below ground she lays?

How come it's easier to feel comfort in pain?
Than to hold on to a happy moment
As if it's stolen before we even get to claim
Making it so much easier to become a loner
In a world which continuously enhances my rage.

They say never loose hope
The sun always comes out after a rainy day
So I find it inside to pray and self-motivate
Trying to accept and understand the laws of the unknown
But, all my self-growth doesn't change what my mind knows
The truth behind what my heart holds and so the question
remains the same.

If smiles are free
How come they're so hard to keep?
How come for me there's always a price to pay?
Whenever I feel one on my face.

Pain

I see you
When I'm putting on my make up, and
I'm trying to cover up how much you enjoy showing off.

I hear you
When you're taking over my thoughts
Hoping I'll stumble some more by
Losing focus while trying to ignore that
You've been knocking at my door all along.

I can taste you
As my choice of words evolve from subtle to rage, and
There's no escaping what I might say
Once those words come out
You get in the way of me turning around
To make amends with the ones I've hurt.

If they only knew how much energy, it takes
To dig up the dirt inside my soul, and
Digest your existence, yet, still I choose
To claim I'm in control and able to keep you at a distance.

I know you
You are the frown that erases my smile instantly
The shadow who darkens my light at the end of the tunnel
The brick walls between me and my blessings
The reason I'm bleeding internally
Teasing as I numb you temporarily

Blocking me from discovering a true remedy
You are my worst enemy.

I feel you
My pain.

Unspoken Words

Unspoken words between me and that man
He knows I'm aware because I'm always dressed
After the fact, when the alarm goes off in the A.M.

I cover any marks left in the end
A bond I wish we never had.

No one asks why I'm always sad
Why I'm always stuck in a faraway land.

I dream of a prince who's stronger than him
I dream of a night when I slept
Without him quietly forcing his body in between my legs
I dream of a day he'll trip, fall and break his neck.

I dream of a night my mom will walk in and catch him in
the act
Yet, she's too busy living a secret life with her best friend.

Too much traumatizing stress for a seven-year-old to have
Maybe I'm better off dead
Better than his sweat all over my fragile flesh
Better than the five dollars a week I get
Better than this painful silence of
Unspoken words between me and that man.

The Monster In My House

A single tear drop falls as I hear the door
The heart of a little girl starting to numb
Knowing what she's about to endure
She lies still as if calm while her mind runs wild
Watching the shadow of the monster that lives in her house.
He's come for more
Again, I must pretend somehow I could sleep through
The coldness and roughness of his hands
Doesn't she ever notice him missing from her bed?
Doesn't she ever get mother's intuition to check?
He spends a lot of time in my room
Do I have a choice?
Is this what all step fathers do?
It's not so bad when he licks
But, the last time he tried to push his private in
Leaving me in excruciating pain like when it hurts to sit
down at school
My hips ache; my thighs shake
It burns so much as he begins; I guess he knows I'm awake
Whispering I need to learn and he's here to teach
So, I take a deep breath confused about the sounds he makes
Afraid to turn around and ask him to please walk out
Yesterday, I heard the big bang as my mother hit the ground
She was crying when he ordered her to stay down
Who will protect us if I yell?
My brothers are young and small
Do I deserve this hell? Is this a curse?
Is this how I'm keeping my mother safe?
So, I'll just lie still and save my siblings from any trouble
Hoping someway I'll live a safer tomorrow.

I Hate These Days

I hate these days when the pain is so great
And I need to hide until I'm done with all the tears
Falling from my eyes.

I hate these days when no matter what I do
I can't take this frown off my face
Feeling like my heart wouldn't survive another mission
Of trying to replace the bad with the good
Of picking up the pieces
Of finding the peace my soul is missing.

I hate these days when I want to scream and shout
I'm mad at others; mad at myself; mad at the world
But, my minds know shouting or pointing the finger won't help
In the end I'll still be stuck dealing with my own inner hell.

I hate these days that test my strength
Making my dreams seem even farther
And just when I think the sadness is over
I realize it just started; I've gone under in my misery again.

I hate these days when I need a friend
But, even as I try to extend my hand for some comfort
I don't have the guts to say, because in reality I wouldn't make any sense
Out of what's going on in my head

Maybe I'm wrong and this is my depression talking
I am the only one who can change the way I woke up this morning
I hate theses days when my all feels like nothing.

Hate

Like dirty laundry; I wish I could wash you away
Using strong chemicals to kill the insane thoughts you create.
Instead, you're a reminder in the back of my mind
Like some display waiting to be bought
Reserving the fact that you know me so much.
Banking on the way that I'm quick to blow up
When my emotions are enslaved by the conclusion I may want
Ignoring the very hard but smart thing to do
Is figure out how to be a part of the solution
Or do nothing at all until I regroup.
But, I have a short fuse called patience
A void which fills itself with aggravation
Revenge has always given me this bitter sweet sensation
Where the disasters of past regrets are not enough
Holding me back from the need of positive inspiration.
Of course, so peacefully right now I can give this Theorell explanation
However, catch me when I'm on fire
When my dirty laundry is out and my smile has expired
When making sure they share my frown, is what matters.
All I see is you inside of me; the way you rush through my veins
Like an addict relapsing every day on
My reactions, and only temporarily satisfaction.
I am weak in the department of understanding
I can't control what others do or say
Instead, I let you make your extravagant entrance
Breaking my walls of love and higher expectations.

Learning to deal with the temptations
What can happen doesn't mean it should
I'm hurting myself every time I include you.
Your definition alone is a red flag; you won't stop till I collapse
A real lesson doesn't exist in your fate
True healing will never take place while keeping you in the equation
And the price to pay, is all of my blessings.
My pain will hold more weight than those I crush
It's a must to erase you from my vocabulary
Your said too often and so fast; written by just four letters
Pure evil, deceitful and too heavy to carry forever
I wish I could wash you away.

The Way I Love You

Looking for a loop
It's all I can do while waiting for the day
Accepted is the way I love you.
Allowing you to laugh at my pain
Allowing you to bash my name
Because, we share the same blood
Running through our veins.
Allowing you to give away my place
Allowing you to claim the stage
Because, the role is being played by my baby boo.
Allowing you to push the knife deeper
Allowing you to think I'm weaker
Because, the real reasons
Are more important than what my anger believes in.
Allowing you to keep me in this prison
Of walls controlled by you teasing
Allowing you to be dissing
The one who granted your existence.
Allowing every cruel step, you take
While I live through others, my baby boo's fate.
Allowing (the key word)
So you never feel the fire that burns
In my soul as I humbly hold the weight.
Allowing, because I choose!!!
Looking for a loop
It's all I can do while waiting for the day
Accepted is the way I love you.

Moments

For what I've noticed so far in life
The feeling of happiness is just moments
Desperate illusions created by ourselves
Illusions that fall like the sun must come down
And the morning awakens yesterday's frown.

A smile is seconds; memories of those moments
Rekindling eventually the inevitable presence
Once night comes back, a tomorrow you're unsure of
And so the years pass you by; all of this is showing
Nothing is real; while holding on trying to steal, a moment.

The So Called Friend

What you thought was weakness on my part
Were moments of me giving you a second chance
To regroup; be a friend and choose your words wisely
Before I start dissecting what you've done from what you said
But instead, you kept spreading your lies and making up
Excuses which made no sense; insulting my intelligence
Overestimating the qualifications of calling yourself my friend.
I will always prefer the truth, even if it hurts; it is what I expect
You thought I'd always bend the rules based on our childhood
Based on when I was too young and ignorant to clearly
see pass
The very manipulative and contradicting personality you have.
Obviously, this is the way your pretend life seems to work
Only feeling good about yourself, when someone else is
doing bad
Executing your cruel plan to continue mentioning my past
mistakes
To whomever will listen; trying to shame my name; hoping
to stain
My accomplishments, with your envious need to cause me
pain.
I have so easily taken the gossip, as another lesson learned
I will not retaliate; my silence and distance will be your
worse regret
If anything, your current situation is the only reason I feel
sad
I will remain being the person who earned every bit of who
I am today

I am not a little girl; the rumors won't change my fate nor slow me down
A path separating me from fake people like you; I used to keep around.

Domestic Violence
(A cycle)

As you can imagine, this section filled with such raw emotions was not easy. This is actually my first step into a near future project necessary to continue with my self-healing. As I type, I'm giving myself a mental hug for undressing my heart in this way for my readers. If my words were to bring forth a lifesaving decision to anyone in a similar situation or creates awareness for the younger generation; everything I survived would not have been in vain. Domestic Violence is not a subject women are eager to admit to, because it makes them feel weak and stupid, especially since people are so quick to judge, gossip or say "I wouldn't stand for this" until it happens to them. In my case it was never a secret, but I'm voicing out the feelings of the numerous amount of women suffering physical abuse behind closed doors confused about still being very much in love with their attacker.

I am very grateful of God's mercy sparing my life numerous times and surrounding me with a very tight, small, yet strong circle of women worthy of admiration. I don't know how I would have seen the light at the end of the tunnel without their unconditional love and support in these very dark moments of my life. They have been my rock in more ways than I can count; our level of trust is rare and there's nothing we can't overcome together (The three musketeers).

If you know someone going through any type of abuse, it is your duty as a fellow woman to help them through a very difficult time; without using their pain for personal entertainment. This section is dedicated to the women who have no one they can express their real feelings to, their thoughts, their pain and their reasons without shame taking over what their lives have become. This is for the women who've died in the hands of their live-in attacker or have died taking such painful memories with them to the grave. As for me, more shall be revealed with time.

The Curse

To stay away from you
I fight my heart every minute of every day.
It's a nightmare preparing my mind all possible ways
So that when we are face to face I maintain the space needed.
A million butterflies begin to rise retrieving my reasons why
Such passion along with your touch, as you apologize
Affects my mental process when it is time to decide
While still knowing somewhere inside how dangerous
Any second your temper may refuse to compromise
Within moments we can go from extremely passionate lovers
To total strangers getting into a fight.

I'm pacing back and forth tormented by the hurtful memories
Of all the physical abuse, tears and lies
I'm not blind; I just can't control the inner desire of believing
That underneath the monster you keep revealing
Resides a soul urging for my healing; so hard to breathe without you
Yet, you can be so deceiving but how do I go against my feelings?
I hear a knock at the door, and there goes my tug of war.
I'll open regardless of the repercussions; regardless of the events
Because, my mind says no but my heart yells, yes.
All confused ass you kiss on my neck; wondering which decision is worse?
Go back and read the first verse.

I Wish

Sometimes I wish I had the power
To simply forget all of our past problems
Or erase my side of the story, but
The reality is, it's gone too far for an "I'm sorry".

Never mind trying to forgive
Pretending I can live with this anger inside, and
Ignore my soul yelling out "girl you better get up and fight".

There's no disguising domestic violence
Unless I plan on hiding from my own life
You've become so unexplainably violent, and
I wasn't built to stay quiet, even if it's to save my own eyes.

Between self-defense, bruises and arguments
There's no room left to be civilized
I wish I had the power to rewind, start again and make
things right
Because, I'm already missing your warm hugs and kisses, but
Reality keeps reminding me there's no fixing someone else's
Way of being or what I'm truly feeling and thinking.

All the love in the world won't change the fact that
I'm risking everything whenever I give you another chance
Wishing doesn't change our situation, and
Praying tells my heart I can do better, because
You've replaced trust with fear; smiles with tears, and
I honestly feel my death near, whenever my prince switches.

A Desperate Plea

I have no energy left, yet
My words express different
While trying to act bold
In front of those who laugh
About the way you explode
Loosing control and lashing out
Beating on me with no remorse
And what scares me the most is
The fact that my heart refuses to
Understand I must let you go.
I don't want to fight anymore
It seems that's all you know or
Want because from the minute
I walk through the door its war
Even as I try to change your mind
Begging you to follow your heart
And protect what we both feel inside
What happened to all the love?
When did the feelings stop?
How come you have to see blood?
Before we go to sleep at night.
I have no energy left
To put my bruises to the side
Just because you refuse to forget
About whatever it was, made us mad.
I'm back hoping to move on, and
Start over again; no questions asked
No reliving a past full of pain
I'm willing to make pretend

The rumors never took place
If you're willing to help me erase
The bad with some good.
I still love you the same
Insanely without regrets
Please get pass this faze, because
I have no energy left.

A Painful Goodbye

This is my hardest task yet
Walking away while still in love with that man
It doesn't hurt less knowing it's the only option I have
I must side with my body and mind ignoring my heart's
replies
If there's any love left for myself inside; if I want to stay
alive.
I have to find the strength to carry on with this decision no
matter what
I have to protect my existence by finally leaving him behind
I have to walk away without saying goodbye face to face
This decision has to be the beginning of ending such a
crucial life.
At corrupting my thoughts, he is the best and always
succeeds
So no warning, not even a letter will be left explaining why.
I've wasted too much precious time waiting for him to
change his ways
And decide to express his love without his constant need
to fight.
I literally risk my all whenever I give him a chance
He cries and begs but once I lay down quietly on our bed
again
His response becomes very dangerous with realistic threats
Of how he'd rather see me dead than not by his side.
A sharp pain in my chest as I grab my bags and take one
last glance
If only we could make things work without bringing out the
worst in each other

If only we could learn to disagree without it escalating into domestic violence
Because, you are also part of my most memorable moments
But, that's just me daydreaming about how it should be
The reality is all the fear involved in this drastic decision
So when in doubt, I'll use my bruises as a reminder of the reasons
To move forward with my hardest task yet
Walking away while still in love with that man.

What Type of Love Is This?

You're forcefully kissing my lips
Lips on a bruised face
Wounds, you will never be able to erase
Even when the black and blues finally fade away.

I stare into your eyes trying to find
The man I fell in love with
The one who always took his sweet time
Making sure I felt safe and satisfied.

Something like, the soft way you're touching me right now
The difference is that our special moments
Became a horror story; a tale I'm ashamed to tell
So I rather hide my face from the world.

Yet, you smile as if we're on a date
As if not so long ago I fought for an escape
Go ahead penetrate against my will
Since obviously you think I'm made of steel.

Licking my bruises hoping it will fix
The moments you replaced your tongue with your fist
While I'm here heartbroken, confused and scared
Still, like a log; holding in my tears
Thinking to myself "what type of love is this?".

Love Slash Threat

Lying on this hospital bed; officers asking me to just shake
my head
When they say your name; showing me pictures of your
lovely face
Telling me over and over again, how you must pay.

I don't want to move a muscle; not only because I love you
But, because I'm still in shock of how it all went down; all I
said was
Maybe it's best we didn't speak for a while; I agreed to
meet one last time
Respecting your right to know my reasons in person;
believing you'd be
Understanding that I no longer felt safe whenever you
were around.

The nurse whispered "try to get some sleep" easier said
than done
Do you have some special kind of morphine to numb a
broken heart?
My thoughts are running wild, wondering how did you
become
The worst part of my present situation; forcing me to find
some place to hide
When just six months ago, you were my Mr. Right.

A nightmare now, that's how it sounds according to the words coming out
My mother's mouth, but how can I demand my mind not to think
How can I stop the flash backs? The memories of you from rushing in
On how it was a dream come true, when we had our first kiss.

The lips that are too swollen now, to ask to be left alone; alone in my shame
Not of us, but ashamed of what took place when I tried to make a stand in defense
When my soul chose to protest, yet, my baby answered with his hands
Where is all the love he claimed to have?

But, I guess this is not about me being able to understand; the reality shows in my scars
I've been brutally abused regardless of who the attacker was, and so with whatever strength
I have left; still in denial of whether or not his attack was out of impulse or planned
Crying because, this is not how I wanted us to end; afraid of what could happen next
I pointed a trembling finger full of regret towards my love slash threat
Pulling the covers over my head; feeling like I had just betrayed my very best friend.

Grief
(Internally Lost)

I've been to many funerals; people I grew up with, cared about and shared memories with passed away. It made me very sad and then you follow suit by reminiscing about your times together. You get drunk with the crew and pour out some of the liquor first out of respect, but the next day you're back to normal. It doesn't happen this way out of cruelty or selfishness; it happens naturally, because you don't truly understand such pain until it hits home.

When my aunt died, it was the first time I was forced to deal with the cruel reality of death. I was a lot younger and already living as a wounded lost soul, but the pain of her death was the icing on the cake for me. I somehow found strength, because I understood it was needed of me whenever I looked into my cousin's eyes, and so I stood strong by their side. I learned life is precious and we're not promised tomorrow; a quote we all say, but saying it and truly understanding the meaning is totally different. As I said before, discussing my aunt creates a suffocating knot, so I will move on quickly. Along with my aunt I buried genuine laughter and walked around with a void until I fell in love.

My relationship with Tito was always on front page, however, I honestly don't care how anyone else felt about our union. Whatever happened between us doesn't take away from our truth, our feelings, our love. When he died, I needed my aunt even more; she would have listened and shared my pain without judging us. I was so lost, heartbroken, empty and found myself trying to numb it all by drinking. I became extremely traumatized by death. I literally died myself emotionally. Thank God I'm a mother, because the love I have for my daughters was the only reason I pulled myself out the hole. However, I did learn the truth behind "God doesn't give you nothing you can't bare" another quote said by many but not entirely understood unless you've been forced by excruciating pain to let go and let God. You honestly don't know how strong you are, until being strong is all you have left.

If you've never gone through something like this, please don't attempt to say "I understand" and the worse thing you can say is "you'll get over it" because it's not true and it is actually a very cruel and thoughtless thing to say. Time does eventually semi heal anything; you learn to live with it, but you never get over it. The best thing you can do is just be there for them by listening. There are many levels to grieving and everyone goes through it differently. Stop judging people's actions, because you have no idea what they are going through inside, of how hard it is to function knowing you will never get an answer no matter how much or how long you cry, asking God why? This section is dedicated to my Tito and to all the people whom are suffering from a loss of a loved one. I pray you find some peace inside, eventually.

Our Story

Our story
Sounds so domestic when memories are spoken of
The listener is probably hoping to hear me say in the end
That I walked away from it all seeking to defend who I am
Ignoring the glow in my eyes as I speak of way back when
Missing the very part of why I feel so broken.
The listener is so caught up in me showing some type of regret
Showing some type of resentment for the way things went
Ignoring the crack in my voice the deeper I get
Into what was then and what was left.
The listener does not see us as a good match
Thinking I should be glad that now we are just a story
Thinking my tears are because I'm reliving bad moments
Ignoring the true reasons, I'm so eager to express
To anyone who's willing to listen about the love I still have.
Our story
Sounds so domestic when memories are spoken of
The listener is ready to start judging
The listener wants to be protective and controlling
On how I should present my version of our story.
The listener takes no notice
On how desperately my heart just needed to be heard
Because, the only curse is being forced
To share my love through memories, and of course
Our story, my words
The daily torture of my truest feelings stuck in my head
Because, if this conversation were about choices
I'd be talking to you instead.

Alone

I feel so alone.
You not being around is like living inside a big black cloud
Full of pain and tears I can't control; decorated with an
everlasting frown
Falling deeper and deeper into a depressive hole,
whenever I imagine myself
Letting go and ripping you out of my heart, mind and soul.

I feel so alone.
Like a star which cannot shine; like a seed not planted right
Like a moon without a night or a sun without a sky to rise
upon
I've been stuck in the lost and found; praying God scrapes
me off the ground
My entire being is in trouble; your love is like a shadow; I
can't see tomorrow
I don't know if I'll ever survive, not having you by my side.

A Second Wind

Breathing is such a mission these days
I wonder how I still function
How I wake up every morning
Force a fake smile on my face
While walking around in so much pain.
The only real sign of life I have is
Hearing them say my name
Asking me over and over if I'm okay.
They can probably see it in my eyes
Any given moment I will break and
Once again scream and cry
Trying to question God on the reason why
He took my baby away.
The insane drive behind my daily quest
Analyzing the tragedy ignoring the facts
Not accepting it's just too late for
Anything I feel I never got the chance to say.
We can't get in the middle of fate
Our time on earth is not our decision to make
Those are the words of reality
Words I can write but can't relay.
The hurt takes priority
Even from working on learning to live
With this empty space of where I used to give
So much strength, hope, forgiveness and sincerity
Now my all is stuck figuring out how to exist.
I am mentally, emotionally and physically drained
Breathing is such a mission theses days
Praying I find my second wind.

A Melt Down

I can cry you a river
But, it won't make a difference
My job is to accept
I will never get the reasons
And need to just feel blessed for being
A part of your life when you were breathing.
Sounds good, right
Beautiful choice of words written
Except this is not another verse to show my skills as a poet
I write instead of loosing my mind and running down the
street
Looking as empty as I feel inside
Every line is full of pain and anger
I should give this poem the title "Disaster"
But, that would mean I've captured all my feelings
When the reality is, I'm nowhere close to healing.

My All

I gave you all I had to give, so now
Happiness between me and someone else will never exist.

Like if after you, nothing could ever be that real
Like if my soul froze the ability to feel.

Every woman dreams, but mine weren't meant to come true
The only man in my dreams has been and will always be you.

Some tell me to try again and live something new, but
I'm trapped in our past and we were stuck like glue.

There's no sense in starting moments doom not to last
I can talk, smile and even hold another's hand, but I
Will never completely let them in, because I gave you all I
had to give.

Just A Breeze

One minute they are here
The next they are gone
The rest are left with so many questions
And answers none
Painful memories of when you could
Reach out to them for a kiss or a hug
Yet the reality is just a breeze
That rushes through your heart
Reminding you of the tragedy
That nearly caused you insanity
Labeling your existence
As a big sign that reads "pause".
Barely breathing from the knot in your throat
What once felt like true love is now
A heavy rock you hold
In the center of your soul
Watching who was so warm and soft
Buried so stiff and cold
It all happens in such a hurry
Physically they are gone
But, emotionally you arte the ghost.
The negative thoughts
Best to be kept untold
Looking on to God
To plant a seed of hope
Praying you get to see them
At least one more time
When it's your turn to go.

The Naked Branch

The season is changing.
This used to be my favorite part
To sit quietly and watch the leaves fall
The naked tree branch
Patiently waiting to be embraced by the snowflakes
As if winter never left.

The same exact way my heart faithfully waits
To be able to smell your cent or hold your hand again
Our faces shinning as bright as the sun on a cold winter night
Staying warm by the insane love burning in our eyes
Lighting up with our smiles the street of South Main
While walking around like the two crazy love birds we were.

Now I wish such natural course didn't take place
All it means is that another year is coming to an end
And I'll be stuck in emptiness, while others celebrate
Asking me to go with the flow and move on from what I
feel inside
Meanwhile emotionally I'm still in summer of 2009.

But, the reality gives me no choice; like in a few months
I'll be forced to store away my gloves and scarfs
And once again the temperature will rise
And my pain frozen in a different time
As the seasons come and go.

My soul is like the naked branch
Patiently waiting to be embraced by the snowflakes
As if winter never left.

Unfallen Tears

I can feel the urge to cry
But, not one single tear has fallen from my eyes.
I know it's necessary, so I can get through tonight
But, my all is literally in shock
My heart stopped pumping truth when I heard the news
Wondering how I'll ever go back to a normal life, without you.
At least when you were doing time there was hope
Letters, visits, phone calls and a promise to meet up no
matter what
Now, the all that's left is this inner fight with my soul
And the last moment I held you close.
My all is prayed out; on stuck mode; my heart hard as stone
So I will write until I have no more words to say
Hoping I don't completely lose control when my silence
breaks
And I can't shake this excruciating amount of pain I hold.
This desire to run away from reality as fast as I can
To a place where I can once again read you my poems
Where you would be able to answer the questions I dread
Why were you put to rest so young?
Why this test to grow old without our love?
Did we destroy the beauty in what we had, fighting?
Did we destroy the chance to be happy by ignoring God's
plans?
Could we have made better choices and avoided this path?
Should we have never laid eyes on each other?
Was it your fate regardless? And if so
How do I get pass the pain and let you go?

I need to know something for sure
Meanwhile I'm unhuman, unalive and torn into small pieces
Of reasons I don't understand; with the urge to cry
But, not one single tear has fallen from my eyes.

Will Time Truly Heal?

I keep praying and giving it to God
Hoping this uncontrollable anxiety
I feel inside will stop
Leaving me in the dark areas of my mind
Filled with empty days and sleepless nights
Scared of breaking down surrendering to the pain
Which, obviously continues to overshadow my life
And right when I think I might have some type of
understanding
The pain presents itself bragging about
How I thought I could dress it up and tuck it away
Afraid to deal with what is in front of my face
Because it's easier to hide or deny
In order to function around what other people have to say
Regarding how much time it should take someone to realize
Loss means they're never coming back no matter how
much you cry.

I keep praying and giving it to God
Confused and tired of looking for ways
To use this pain as another experience
When in reality I'm grieving like if he died today
The only difference is that instead of just numbing, I pray
Annoyed by those who tell me "it's going to be okay" or "I
feel you"
I'm intelligent and spiritual enough to know what doesn't
kill you
Makes you stronger

And you couldn't possibly feel my pain unless you share the story of
Burying your lover
Save the words which are so easy to say when you get to go home and
Lay in bed with your significant other
Show some respect for my pain or don't even bother
My rage has no boundaries when I'm this down and under.

I keep praying and giving it to god
As a reminder that it's no one else's fault
I research grief and psychoanalyze each stage I may be active on
In faith of God's promise to heal
Because in the midst of it all the only thing I know for a fact
Is yesterday's unexplainable truth which is still so real today, and
This is how my prayer starts, "God you know I love me some Tito".

A Ticking Bomb

I'm a ticking bomb that's been thrown
On the ground ticking but not allowed to explode.
It's like an anxiety attack that never goes away
A soul still eager to fight for the rights of a love
A love which died and now is lost
Lost in the depths of my inner denial slash rage.
At times I can come across as a contempt and calm danger
zone
But, when my soul gets tired of functioning on sleep mode
And my heart is awake demanding to feel alive
Please don't try to console or expect warmth from a cold
place
While my heart is forced to once again realize
The reasons why it's best to remain alone.
A solution for my inner rage isn't humanly possible
A rage that multiplies as the years go by
This amount of pain must be kept between God and I
A bomb God will have to personally shut off
A bomb you will never be able to disarm.
Stuck on his love with no batteries attached and unwilling
to talk
There's no invitation to this intervention
As selfish as it might sound; this situation only has to do
with my life
When my depression is going round and round in my mind
My heart and soul refuses to compromise
And the more dangerous it becomes, for whoever is trying
to get inside.
Inside of this ticking bomb wanting vengeance

Hoping to someday let go or grow into acceptance.
A growth which is not yours to supervise
Unless you want to always bare witness whenever my
heart chooses to rewind
To all it naturally knows, which are my true feelings.
You should not get involved with my process of healing
It is not your job to erase or seek replacement
This is not a game; this is a bomb full of resentments.
Don't set yourself up for the ugly version
I'm not programmed to stop when my all is hurting.
I'm a bomb that's been thrown
On the ground ticking but not allowed to explode.

Dear Heart

I'm writing you this letter
Hoping we'll work together
At helping our soul feel a little bit better.

We need to start seeing eye to eye
We can continue to cry and drive ourselves insane
We can continue to ask why but it won't change the facts
The unanswered questions will remain just that.

We've tried it all
We've exhausted the mind trying to find some unrealistic answer
Just to feed our thirst for his love.

I have stood by your side faithfully
Holding on to someone we will never speak to again or touch
I know we went as far as tattooing our forever promise
And usually I won't let anything or anyone bother us in our mission
To be imprisoned with our feelings and thoughts
But, we are not eating or sleeping and soon
We won't have the strength to even talk.

We can explain our pain until the end
We can write a book to cope with his death
We can swear to never forget the moments spent
We can hold our memories sacred
This is not about truly letting him go

But, we must accept he's gone
Even if acceptance is a reminder of being alone
Because, he would want us to be strong
I'm not asking you to pretend; I know we need to mourn
But, how about if we agree to move on from this self-
destructive faze
And stand tall along our love and yesterday's memories
Learning to live for today.

The Rooms
(A Self Inventory)

No matter how many blunts I smoked or bottles of Bacardi Lemon I drank, I realized it wasn't enough to numb my pain. There was so much anger accumulated inside, so many days wasted laying in bed trying to find purpose; a new reason to live. Suicide was never an option and I owe those beliefs to my mother who introduced me to God as a child, engraving in my soul "taking your own life is one of the worse sins". However, there were many nights I cried myself to sleep begging God to take me with him. I would wake up the next day upset; now I thank God everyday for ignoring such ignorance. I needed something different fast; I'm fully aware of what my reality could have become had I, like so many others, taken the easy route and graduated into a different type of drug, but instead I chose to call my brother.

My brother introduced me to the rooms. Thank God he was strong enough to change his life around and become a positive example not only for our family, but for all the hopeless souls he inspires when he shares his story. At first I just didn't want to hurt anymore. I had lost control of my life. My final rock bottom was burying Tito (grateful for growing into such understanding) because looking back throughout my life I had plenty of turning points, yet, chose to ignore, numb and blame others. The rooms forced me to take self-inventory and take responsibility for my actions; had I not followed through, I wouldn't be publishing my first book today. I would've still been writing because it's my passion, but not doing anything with it; we are our worst enemy.

I thought I'd smoke weed and drink forever. It still crosses my mind from time to time, because dealing with raw emotions is not easy, but in the rooms I learned it's about the choices you make and I chose growth. Addiction is real and can be deadly on any level. I lost so many loved ones to drugs; I still cry about it and wonder if they were ever introduced to the rooms. The rooms gave me the tools I needed to live a better and healthier life, so I will never be ashamed to mention something so meaningful and positive, especially if this section can help save a life.

I dedicate this section to those who made it easier for me to admit my life had become unmanageable due to drugs by sharing their story, struggle and advise. To those who work hard every day to keep the meetings going so someone like me had a place to share pain and urges without being judged. To those who are up all night for the anonymous phone lines, who visit halfway houses and institutions genuinely giving back. Thank you for all the hugs and life saving memories. Thank you for teaching me how to have a personal relationship with God. May God continue blessing you all.

The Pretenders

At 1:45am the lights come back on
Last call for alcohol; the show is over
The stage starts getting cleaned up
For whoever wants to escape again
To a night full of temporary smiles and fun
All you have to do is get drunk or your drug of choice
No matter which one; you will enjoy.

Everyone here is on cloud nine
Where all your lies shine bright for the right price
Too bad that, regardless of much you spend
How much you pretend or the amount of fake friends
you make
You can't truly erase what you feel inside.

The details you left untold; those details called "your real
life"
You can park your true feelings outside; for your
performance
You can indulge in your lies or be the one lonely sitting in
the corner
Quiet, as if in control; playing the worse role of them all
The one who at the end explodes
Some don't know their place once the curtain closes
And the pain begins; soon you will be sober.

At 1:45am the lights come back on
Last call for alcohol; the show is over
The stage starts getting cleaned up
For whoever wants to escape again
To a night full of temporary smiles and fun.

A Self-Inflicted Disease

I did not want to see
How much you were hurting me
Besides a piece of paper and pen
For years you were my best friend.
Using your company to hold back my tears
Thinking that by numbing my pain and fears
I would never mentally or emotionally fall
I did not want to see
You were part of what was wrong.
You were where I ran
When I felt no one else could understand
Protected you and enabled you to define who I am.
Always found an excuse to bring my problems to you
For you I'd fight refusing to say goodbye
Maybe because you've been in my life since I was young.
Thought we'd grow old together
Thought you would keep me bold and strong forever
The brick wall I helped you build
Empowering the big lie that was I
Existed only to never let me heal
Separating me from what I truly feel.
Staying drunk and high made me closed minded and blind
I did not want to see
The need to let out and cry
So I could finally set myself free
Rescuing my soul from being self-centered and weak
You were blocking me mentally from what I now know.
You are a self-inflicted disease
You are an option, not a must; the suffering can simply stop
As long as I choose not to pick up.

Obvious Reservation

My principles are against you
Yet, subconsciously I wish you'd sneak up on me.
This inner need to forget at least for a while
Even if in the end I'm full of regret and on trial
On trial over the lifestyle I no longer wanted to extend.
The jury constantly reminds me of way back when
The prosecutor and judge both battle it out in my head.
On the stand is my spirit grieving emotions I can't control
The evidence is the stress that shows, instead of
My soul dealing with the threats of ignorance
There's a price to pay when you finally know
Even, if the committee in your mind tries to tell you different.
I honestly fell in love with my clean date, and
Understand the decisions I make will forever hold
What I say, said, tell and told.
But, mental growth can feel a bit overwhelming
Especially when I'm not sharing my truest thoughts
Every day it feels harder to spread positive energy
If deep down reacting negatively has a deeper urgency.
The rooms are like the media watching my every step
Getting more and more time will help me look at my best
But you are the only shadow I see clapping
Laughing at the good in me leaving a meeting
Walking home with the heavy load of conscious
Trying to pretend you don't glow like the excitement
I've been missing for so long.
I'm tired of being strong, bored and alone
Not that this wasn't the case before, but
Before I didn't have to mentally attend court

Before I played the fifth and ignored
Now, it's always in my face every second of every day
And it all takes place inside of me
This spiritual war of right or wrong.
My principles are against you
Yet, subconsciously I wish you'd sneak up on me
So I can play the victim and accidently trip into a situation
Where I can come up with a good enough excuse
Of why I went through with this obvious reservation
And so the fight continues
My heart knows I need to talk about it
My mind remains silent entertaining the secret invitation.

The Walls of Recovery

At times it feels like the walls of recovery are closing in
Leaving me without space to take a step back and breathe
Like if regardless of how much I pray for sanity
My thoughts reveal the emptiness of my reality.

At times the anxiety of living a full recovery
Pulls me away from the new strategy
Of focusing on my accomplishments
Leaving me with nothing but acknowledgements of my
failures
As I catch myself constantly stumbling.

At times the truth of this program
Goes against my regrets and endless moments of anger
When all I have to hold on to is what I'm forced to
remember.

At times past tense seems easier than this crazy adventure
Healing without physical medication
Leaving my thoughts or as they say "disease"
Without being able to internally escape can be very
depressing.

Learning to find a solution by prayer and meditation
But, I guess this is the realness involved with the pressure
Of finally being a part of the race in achieving becoming a
better person.

The Rise of Beatriz

This war began long ago
Even though for years each individual battle froze
And until now, the reasons were still unclear and untold
Since I can finally feel every single blow.
Instead of hiding in the shadow of fearing the unknown
I now have a date and a place for all of my painful episodes
Now they're all willingly embraced
Even though it forced me to face the side I hate to
personally know.
Someone I must turn around to save
While battling inside the urge to send it all to hell
That hell is my home, what we also call our brain or our souls
I have no choice but to mingle with the hurt and shame
And mold the remains into inner hope
Hoping someday I'll be completely okay with the ghost
Of a past I can't understand or explain.
Making amends; trying to experience peace and space
For the person I dream about being today, because an
escape
Should be forever erased from my options
It's just too late to retract
Or waste more time sucked in by the demon of regret
I'm too grown to be placed for adoption.
This war began long ago
Since everything in my life kept adding up to an improper
fraction
I will divide and subtract until I make sense of everything
that happened
Trying to leave alone and behind whatever shouldn't matter

Like all the blows I somehow survived
Until my insides surrender and Betty Boo waves the
white flag
So Beatriz Velez is able to rise.

Yesterday

The resentment and pain had taken over my ways
I was lost in my own skin fighting to find a place
Where I could breathe for a minute and think.
I wanted to escape who I'd become
I wanted to run away from everything I saw wrong
Especially from the decisions I continued to make
Based on the reactions of a broken heart
I knew I still existed only because
My eyes would open wide to the rise of the sun
Yet there I'd remain numb to life
Waiting for the moon and the stars
Hoping it would be my last night.
I just couldn't come up with a reason why
I was worthy of being alive
Surrounded by so many negative thoughts
My soul felt stuck for good
I figured I'd lived enough.
Tired of being misunderstood
With absolutely no one I could trust
Was when I prayed telling God I was done
To take whatever is left of me and do whatever he wants
Was when yesterday ended and today begun.

Today

The resentment and pain gives true meaning to my new ways
I am content with who I am and God's purpose with my past
I know God's plan for me is better than what I can imagine
I am worthy of a second chance
Regardless of any regrets I may have or the tragedies that happened.
I can stand and meditate peacefully about my next step
I love that I'm a working progress to make things right
I accepted that as human I will hurt and cry
But I can choose to not allow my feelings consume my life.
The rest will eventually fall into place along with complete healing
There's really no need for others to understand, because God's approval is all I ever needed.
So I start my days smiling at the sun grateful for his grace
And fall asleep appreciating the gift to see the moon and the stars with faith
That God will carry me when times get rough
As long as I continue to pray and trust
That the devil is a liar
That yesterday ended and today has begun.

My Higher Power
(The almighty God)

I will always be grateful to my mother for planting the seed of God in my life as a child, because as a parent I understand the importance in teaching our children about the creator. In the midst of the storm of my childhood, I did grow up with a conscious, thanks to my genuine fear of God. I made so many mistakes and there were times blinded by the trials and tribulations when I questioned "Is there really a God?" and if there is "why did he bring me into this world to suffer so much?". Once I finally cleared my mind, I realized God never left my side, it was I who lost faith.

I thank God for having mercy on my soul, allowing me to carry on my duties as a mother, allowing me to meet and enjoy my granddaughters; since I now have a deep understanding that every breath I take is someone else's last. I will forever be grateful; my youngest daughter is a cancer survivor and I survived the streets without any visible scars or incarceration. I walk proudly with a limp (the doctor's said I'd never walk again). I suffer from chronic migraines and P.T.S.D. due to Domestic Violence, but I'm alive.

I also stopped pointing the finger at everybody else and took a good look at myself, the choices I made, the consequences I caused, how selfish I was, all the negativity I was spreading. The power of words is amazing; you can literally make or break someone with your words. I am a working progress but at least I acknowledge my wrongs and through the power of prayer I have found peace in my heart and the strength to help those who feel like I once felt, broken and lost. This is not about religion, because religion is man-made, this is about having your own personal relationship with God, this is about teaching others the power in prayer, this is about finding your true purpose in life.

This section is the most important one in my heart, my life and my truth. This section is dedicated to the only one who loves me unconditionally, has never left my side and has never turned his back on me. To the one who protected my children when I was up to no good and has allowed me to experience this childhood dream. I thank you and ask you God to bless my readers and have mercy on their souls as well as mine.

Realization

Drowning in my pain, losses and non-disguisable frown
Sitting there brokenhearted but tired of sitting my life out
Allowing my existence to settle for just being a witness
Of my uncontrollable feelings going round and round
Without a solution or destination
Without my mind or pride willing to question
I had become a shadow of my own situation
So I had to spiritually separate me from myself.
Finally giving my soul a chance to take a look around
I saw my heart in pieces scattered all over the ground
I saw footprints of my impulsive decisions
The ones I hoped would lift my soul
Were actually the ones shoving my spirit deeper into a hole
I saw a girl who had never been afraid of standing alone
Crushed, lost and avoiding any new loads
Refusing to walk through the path of acceptance
Refusing to view anything as a blessing
I saw a girl ready to forfeit the fight
The same girl who usually used any challenges as a bridge
To get her to the other side and win
Not thinking twice of the battles which lied ahead
Not worried about what she might face in the end.
I couldn't believe she was done; the one who always had
a plan!
So I became desperate, anxious for answers
On how to re-create and start this thing called my life, again
I spoke to the most intelligent people I had ever met
But nothing they suggested made any sense
I needed something more powerful than intellect

And medicating myself would just put me to rest
Leaving me still there clueless and depress
My last resort was asking God for a hint
Admitting I was powerless to all I held within.
And all of a sudden the wind blew stronger
With just a few honest words
Humility and acceptance was a well-deserved lesson learned.
I felt this urge to want to live
And all of my problems instantly seemed smaller.
Through prayer was when the realization began
I had tortured myself all along
Instead of putting it all in God's hands.

My Spiritual War

Being followed ever since I could remember
Running was pretty much usually the answer
Years of darkness taking pleasure
Demons in creepy laughter giving me a head start
Excitedly watching from afar how I would self-destruct.
In fear of how lost and cold my soul had become
Viewing righteousness like an old and boring song
I continued feeding my pain; siding with the dark
An obsessed masochist; crying, yet, allowing them
To steal potential moments of peace and happiness
Walking in the shoes of a lonely sinner's broken heart.
I couldn't see a way out of looking over my shoulders
Stressing the nightmares of the daily dreadful attacks
There's a spiritual war going on for our souls since we
were born
This is not a conspiracy theory; these are facts!!
Half of the torture are my own inner doubts
Bad decisions I made which I could never take back
And if you don't know the importance of cleansing your soul
You're spiritually completely gone and no longer a threat.
In the end, what will you say for yourself on judgment day
The devil's secret weapon is making you feel too ashamed
To find the strength to face your demons head on
To understand the difference between a fake smile and a
natural glow
The difference between my true purpose in life and a
common goal
The difference between multiplying my accounts or
spiritual growth

The difference between negative or positive ambitions.
These demons are on a mission to toy with my dreams and feelings
However, the minute I acknowledged their existence and hold
I also understood I didn't have to fight alone, and so I surrendered
To a power greater than my pain and deceitful ways
Were I found comfort in God's protection, true love and blessings.

Faith

Why do I ignore this feeling in my heart?
The reminder of everything starts and ends with you
The inner voice confirming you're always around
Anxious to erase my frown and make all things new.
Why do I ignore the facts?
The heavy load of pain I carry inside every day
My worries, fear and tears I try so hard to hide away
While you're always there patiently waiting to create a path
A reality, from which I no longer feel the need to escape.
Why do I remain so cold, dwelling on the sadness in my soul?
Making my life extra complicated as if I didn't know
Without you by my side there's no winning chance
All it takes is one true breath of faith, and instantly the light
Of your incomparable love can change for the best, my fate
Instead of this band aide I'm forced to daily replace
For holding on to ignorant pride instead of holding on to
my faith.

God Lives Within

So much fighting in different parts of the world
Who is God, and what's his real name?
Which day will he come, and what religion will he save?
Forcing the ones who are truly lost to slip away
Instead of guiding them into a spiritual path of
Finding the love of God within; in their own way
To eventually change their lives and cleanse their sins.
Those who are not open-minded enough to know
You can enjoy a relationship with God even if you're
praying home alone
Can literally go insane trying to live up to someone else's
righteous ways
The ten commandments clearly explain what we should
aim for
It is an individual journey for each and one of us, and only
God decides
Who will rise and who will stay, so watch out for the many
corrupted minds
Making you think they are the way to a path that's only
yours to find.
Live your life to the fullest; without loosing yourself on the
ride
All the answers to your deepest questions are all inside
Just ask your heart if so far you're worthy of salvation
And if your heart says, you're not, then analyze your
mistakes
Creating a testimony out of your own lessons will become
your true blessing
There's nothing like when you willingly surrender

There's nothing like when your soul can hear God's voice
The bible clearly states; not even the angels know the date
Your personal bond with God will come from within; not
from a particular religion
The rest remains untold until the arrival of our creator on
judgment day.

Put All Your Trust in God

I trust you lord with all my heart
Not because I'm supposed to
Not because it's the right thing to say or do
But, because you've proven the unconditional love
You have for me in numerous ways; meanwhile others
quickly walked away.

They will break promises and overlook my pain
They will change their opinions based on what I gave
yesterday
Not what I can afford to give today
They will claim to be faithful without wanting to hear
What my tears or melt downs are trying to say
And be the first to turn around and hurt you; if they have
nothing to gain.

Yet, through each and every hurtful and challenging stage
Which took place in my life; you're the only one who never
left my side
Your unconditional love and grace shines brighter than
the sun
I will be eternally grateful for having someone I can trust.

Internal Growth

When I analyze my past
I'm not proud of the choices I made
It's not like I secretly smile about it
Or childishly think I was the boldest chic around
Whenever I mentally hit replay
There are episodes that still to this day cause an
excruciating frown
The loved ones I've hurt, especially the ones who are no
longer around.
I'm not too prideful to admit where we went wrong, and
It's a torment in itself knowing I can't change what went on
All I can do is focus on never making those same mistakes.
Praying my actions today may in some way reflect as proof
and show
How genuinely sorry I am and as long as I live
I will continue to do for others, hoping there's this
enormous amount of good
Powerful enough to erase the bad or at least evenly
balance my soul.
A very humbled soul from carrying the heavy load of regret
An understanding soul who knows not to expect
forgiveness
But, a grateful soul for awareness of my sins and evil acts.
When I analyze my past
I'm not proud of the choices I made
But, I thank God for the guidance and wisdom to write this
poem
And throughout these honest words flows not only my shame
But, also God's merciful grace to help heal my pain
As I embrace his opportunity of internal growth.

Dare to Be Different

The more I research, the more it hurts
Realizing all I believed in is some wicked curse
Created to keep us trapped in our flesh's desires
To quench this thirst, we go against our father.
Selling our souls just to climb the ladder
Designed as a deadly path for the blind
While they sit on the sidelines in laughter
Watching us fight one another.
Millions have died giving value to their dollar
Our children we sacrifice if we don't strive
To break away and deny what this cruel world has to offer
And focus on what truly matters
The beautiful gift God blessed us with called, life.
It's even worse once you've opened your eyes
We will be held accountable based on our knowledge
Some are genuinely ignorant acting out a false reality
Naturally rehearsed from birth
Caught up in the position of a follower
Unaware of what's really going to happen after
And so what's done to them they do to others.
It's a domino effect but some are given the power
To understand the hand, they've been served
And if I haven't lost you yet with these words
Then you are responsible for whatever happens
To those around you if you remain quiet
The voice inside you choose to ignore
Is God warning you of what's behind that door
Don't be the one with no return
Allowing the demons of envy and greed

Leave you soulless in these streets
Don't seal the deal in blood seeking success
Chasing the American dream or nightmare from where I see
Don't wait until it's too late
And you are left, with the rest, in the darkness of regret
Be the first to admit we must pick a side
And invest your heart, soul and mind into the only one
Who loves you for who you truly are
The only one who can promise us a better future
Be patient and the blessings will come with interest
Be a real trooper, be a soldier of God
Dare to be different.

Anything for You

"Catherine I miss you" he yelled, with those puppy brown eyes and fragile wrinkle on his forehead when he's mentally waving his white flag; humbly making his presence known, while fearlessly demanding my attention. He stands there alone surrounded by people who hate him, confident I won't let them hurt him, because I love him so, and they love me. We know it all boils down to how we feel about each other, and the proof is in the cocky secret smirk as we admire one another. However, the pressure once again is on me; the tension to pick between my family and the man I love. Where they see weakness I see feelings. Where they see distraction I see adventure. Where they see my doom I see my future, because while they seek an end to it all I seek, hope for, wish and desire a true beginning full of the amazing love we share when we are at peace.

Everyone is waiting for my response; meanwhile I'm internally struggling against the urge to yell back how much I've missed him too. Looking deep into his eyes reminds me of someone I know. We share the same puffiness of no sleep and crying all night forced to change our daily routine. It's only been two days they say, but when you're in love one day apart feels like eternity. He winked at me and said "you know where I'll be". I quickly turned my face knowing how just a wink from his very seductive and mysterious brown eyes makes my heart skip a beat. I am completely powerless to his touch; to his style of affection. I should hate him right now, but I don't. where they see a monster I see my baby. As usual I ignored their comments and left in a hurry; all I can think about is the pain I saw in his eyes. I can't wait to kiss him, hug him, touch him and comfort him.

I was walking with a smile on my face reminiscing of how wonderful our moments together are when neither one of us is mad. I felt the excitement of a woman rushing to reunite with the man she loves. I was daydreaming of all the endless possibilities if we could just focus on making each other happy. Yet, the fairy tale came to an end as soon as I reached those same cement steps which scrapped my chin as I fell trying to escape him two days ago. My smile switched to a frown and tears dropped with a deep understanding of how fast our dream becomes a nightmare. However, it didn't stop me from going up the stairs, because the obsession inside my heart to be near him, to feel his warmth is stronger than the fear of reliving the nightmare.

The neighbor's approached me puzzled as I stepped into the hall way "Are you okay?" they asked. I could tell they were afraid for me and I did feel embarrassed about the whole situation, but I was determined to see my baby. The hall way leading to my apartment door is very small, but it felt like the longest walk ever. A walk of shame and guilt over my own actions, but there was no turning back. I can't explain this love; all I know is I can't live without him. Any shrink would diagnose me insane for returning to the crime scene full of bruises. I used to be so damn prideful but the minute I put my guard down he took over my world. I can honestly admit to myself the thought of never seeing him again hurts more than any physical abuse, and so I quickly gathered my thoughts and very softly knocked on the door.

Our secret knock; my brother is looking for him and he's one family member who will have no mercy on my baby, and yes no keys. No keys to an apartment I rented three weeks ago after working my ass off so we can have a place of our own. A home which shortly after we moved in became a horror story; more reasons for my family and those who entertain themselves with my agony to talk. Yet, it never fails; one kiss from the prince and my judgment holds no weight against the way he makes me feel. His touch is like magic, so before any words were said I was hypnotized by his tongue and his muscular body over powering my every move. He seduces me like no other and takes no prisoners when he's trying to blow my mind. Make up sex is the best even if he's licking the bruises he caused.

We went at it for hours expressing with our bodies how much we've missed and love each other. Body language is the only form of communication which exists between us where no fights occur, complaints or disappointments. Inside our bubble it felt like heaven; butt naked lying down cuddling with my baby while he caresses my back. If only they could witness when he treats me like a queen. Aside from the bad, our good moments are filled with the most memorable moments in my life. He made me something to eat so we could regain our energy. Round two, round three; a bubble bath relaxing our muscles and just when I was about to pass out the questions began, "Catherine, where did you stay?" "Who were you with?" "I looked for you everywhere".

At first a profound silence took over me, because I know the look behind the smile all so well, but still I tried to work around it and salvage our special moment. I kissed him softly and told him I stayed at my friend's house. He starred at me for a long time anxiously waiting for me to give a different answer. I began to feel uncomfortable and mad; there he was again turning a beautiful moment into an awkward and negative situation. I could see those veins popping out of the side of his neck when he gets extremely upset, so I asked him to please stop trying to make something out of nothing. He should know better by now; we are both short tempered. It doesn't take much to get me going and still I tried to avoid the fight by explaining in detail just like he likes it, my whereabouts minute by minute how I was able to hide for two days. I was willing to say everything except where, which infuriated him even more, but I was not going to include my friends in our drama.

"You think it's Funny?" my baby in a very devious voice. "No" I answered, in my I can't believe you're taking it there voice. Damn, doesn't he get it? I just didn't have the energy to fight anymore and needed some time to myself, I needed to feel safe. I was hiding because of him and here he is squeezing the hell out of my hand demanding an answer. Fuck why I was hiding, all he cares about is where. I had to open up to my friends, swear them to secrecy and involve them into my bullshit because I had no where else to go. I didn't want my family to see me with a swollen face. I didn't want to hear I told you so. My eyes started to tear unsure if it was out of anger or the reminder of the big hole in my heart from the invincible knife he continues to dig deeper. He walked away and entered the bathroom so I figured I could finally relax and get out of attack mode. I heard him taking a piss so I laid back down hoping afterwards we could take a nap together and put this nonsense of his crazy jealousy to rest. I hadn't closed my eyes completely when I was lifted off the sofa by my hair.

"Who were you with for the pass two days?" he kept yelling as he dragged me naked all over the living room floor. "Please stop" is all I could say while trying to cover my knees from the severe rug burns trying to balance so I could stand on my feet. I knew he wasn't going to stop, he never did. Mixed emotions of not feeling surprised at all by his actions and at the same time not understanding why he would go through the whole motion of making love to me, to then hurt me? Its painful and traumatizing to even wonder if this was his plan all along. How could he question why I hid knowing he didn't give me any other choice? I hate having to plot on the man I love in order to defend myself. The only thing I was able to grab was the remote control; I hit him in the face as hard I could and so he swung me against the wall with all his might.

My face hit the wall, coffee table and floor within seconds; my tooth ripped through my lip and blood stained the rug. I looked up and saw him coming towards me with a bloody nose. "Baby stop" I begged, but he was starring at me like if I was his worse enemy. I was afraid; not only about what could happen to me, but also about what I was capable of doing to him. I tried to run for my clothes, but he man handled me down to the ground and put his legs on my arms so I couldn't move. Scared and heartbroken, I was still willing to talk if he would just stop. I love him so much; any type of kind gesture on his part right now would erase it all, but my prince was too busy trying to literally take my breath away. He wrapped his arms around my neck squeezing harder and harder as he whispered his love for me was so deep he'd rather kill me and himself than to see me with anyone else.

I wanted to tell him he's all I think about; how my heart, mind and soul belong to him but the room was getting darker. I could feel my life slipping away. I could hear my soul desperately asking God for help, as I woke up drenched in sweat. You'd think my first thoughts realizing it was just a dream would be thanking God I was alive and safe, but instead I curled up in fetal position hysterically crying until the sun shined through the window. These damn nightmares of a past I'd relive again without thinking about it twice just to feel him next to me one more time. My present state of mind hurts more; stuck here alone with my thoughts and memories trying to find ways to function in his absence. I have questioned many episodes and am fully aware of the type of danger I was in, but as crazy as most people may think I sound; there are no regrets on my behalf. We promised forever no matter who, no matter what.

"Catherine, are you okay?" my rock asked. I call her my rock because hers are the only words making any sense to me as I wait to meet with him for the last time. I'm grateful to have such a beautiful soul in my corner who has offered her home so I can cry in private and at a distance from those eager to give their opinion. The best part of my rock is she's been here before and so she knows when to approach me and when it's best to just let me be. Usually, I'm all for confrontation, especially if they are trying to speak on my baby in a negative way, but these days getting out of bed is a challenge. The little energy I do have is used to pour myself another glass of Bacardi Lemon and roll up to ease the panic attacks.

I looked to the side and stared at a pile of crumbled papers from me trying to write my feelings down. Writing has been my escape ever since I was a little girl, but how do you escape from inside yourself? I wanted so bad to trade places with anyone else in the world or not exist, but after guzzling half the bottle; the false peace of drunkenness and numbness appeared. I even giggled envisioning him being a pain in my ass demanding to know my every thought. A bottle of Bacardi and a whole box of cigarettes later left me passed out with the pen in my hand and a notebook full of the first words my soul was willing to reveal:

I really don't know where to start. How do you begin a story where you dread writing the ending? I've ripped it up a million times, only to start all over again so I can mentally stay where it all began. Maybe its best I stay stuck in the beginning, maybe its easier to rewind when you're being forced against your own will to move on. These words will not bring him back to me or take my pain away, but it always made me feel happy when writing about us. I hope my theory is right, by keeping my promise and telling our story will work as some type of therapy. Our forever promise must be shared with the whole world. Have you ever felt like you've known someone your whole life in a short period of time? Have you ever been a hundred percent sure he's the one you've been waiting for? Have you ever felt like that someone completes you? I grew up listening to my aunt talk for hours about the love of her life and her eyes would shine bright as she spoke; such natural glow. She told me this type of love only happens once. I was also aware of the old family gossip regarding her prince, but my aunt would make the craziest story sound like the most romantic moments ever. She told the same stories for years, with the same amount of excitement each time and God forbids anyone had anything negative to say about her prince. Her stories never bored me; I imagined what it would be like to be so romantically involved. Aside from her stories, I had never experienced true romance for myself. I knew about having love for someone but nothing about being head over heels in love, and definitely not about someone being head over heels in love with me and not being afraid to show it. My aunt told me it happens naturally, and when it did I'd know; I would feel it deep in my soul when I met the one. I remember telling him like it was yesterday how I could write a book about our love and if God permits it I don't want to leave this earth without keeping my promise. "A Forever Promise" tattooed on my lower back years ago as proof of no matter what happened between us, in my life he would forever be known as my soul mate. Have you ever met your one? What do you believe your one should be like? The one can mean something different to each of us individually but for me the one was he who had the power to steal my heart unexpectedly like a thief in the night. The one you know you belong to, not because they say so but because you feel it. Your love for the one is something you can't control. You probably have kicked your one out a bunch of times and then stayed up waiting and hoping they return. The one who makes you say yes, when the answer should be no, and not because he's forcing you, it's the emotional trip you take when starring into his eyes; destination anywhere as long as you wake up in his arms; the one who can crumble your world with his words and erase it all with a kiss. The one you would give your last to even if they didn't deserve it. The one you trust with your life even if all you guys do is fight, the one when if you're wrong then you don't want to be right. You might think my definition of the one is nuts but that's okay, because that's exactly how you love the one, in a nutty way. Not one night, episode or promise was ever planned, it was spur of the moment from the moment we dared to look in each other's eyes. Do you believe in love at first sight?

About The Author

My name is Beatriz Velez. I was born in South Norwalk, CT (nicknamed Betty Boo). I am the middle child out of five raised by a single mother in a very noisy household. As you can imagine, many things were taken from me and privacy was no exception. My only possessions were my thoughts so I spent most of my early years writing my feelings down. In school, I always loved reading and writing. I was always particularly interested in finding out about the author and would create a story behind the story of the writer's life. During my teenage years and early twenties, a piece of paper and pen at times were my only two real friends when the chaos surrounded me. For many years, my audience consisted only of my inner circle (certain friends and cousins) but there was the pleasure of occasional strangers, whom you'll probably never see again. One of my cousins always advised me to take my writing more seriously, but I am my worse critic. However, I realized that I have a gift to express myself with beautifully selected words, and I could also be inspired by what others shared with me. My poetry is no walk in the park. My poetry is the voice of a soul, who has lived many different lives, pain, loss, heartbreak, ect. My poetry, as well as my books, is all based on true stories. I have been writing my entire life; yet, I gave up on the silent childhood dream of being a well-known and acknowledged writer, my true passion. It wasn't until my loss and hitting rock-bottom when I truly challenged myself as a professional writer. Raw Emotions is only the beginning. More shall be revealed because the more I wrote, the more I healed. I thank God for every set-back, for every obstacle and for every single tear. I am a living example of what one can accomplish with faith and determination. I whole heartedly thank you for contributing to my dream and listening to my story.

CPSIA information can be obtained
at www.ICGtesting.com
Printed in the USA
FFOW03n0838030118
44280667-43840FF